Praise for *Virtual Reality For Main Street*

"Kudos to Todd Brinkman for writing *Virtual Reality for Main Street*. Although virtual reality is cutting edge technology that has established itself through video games, Todd introduces it in a way that is approachable and accessible to everyone. His exploration of creative applications of VR and 360 video for use in therapy, education, personal historical documentation and for simply creating joy will inspire readers to utilize this transformative technology to benefit their own lives and their communities."

Aaron Brossoit
CEO of Golden Shovel Agency and PlaceVR

"*Virtual Reality for Main Street* is a simple approach to understanding VR that encourages the reader to digest/consider how this life-changing technology can advance humanity by bringing new examples of access to knowledge and systems, especially in training and education, that will move humanity forward during this 4th Industrial Revolution."

Ed Hidalgo
Chief Innovation and Engagement Officer
Cajon Valley Union School District

"If you're feeling disconnected in today's complicated world, this well-organized book *Virtual Reality for Main Street* introduces a fascinating solution. While the potential use cases span many diverse industries, I personally feel this technology introduced into the healthcare arena could radically improve the quality and humanity of medical care today. I fully support this movement and look forward to seeing what unfolds!"

Janet Bruno, M.D.
Executive in Residence
W.P. Carey School of Business, Arizona State University

"Brinkman's commitment to creating virtual reality experiences for families, organizations, senior facilities, and churches is inspiring. This innovative way of connecting dissolves barriers and paves new neuropathways of love, unity, creativity, and compassion. The way of the future!"

Christine Gail
CEO Unleash Your Rising
Best-selling Author, Leadership Strategist, Book Publishing

"Business leaders, if I showed you a new innovative strategy to help your team excel to the next level, emerge and redefine the workspace would the strategy be worth your effort? I read Todd's new book, *Virtual Reality for Main Street*. He has developed a definitive strategy to show you exactly how to turn your team's personal dreams into a 360 experience and feel as if they have already won! Read this book. Every leader should have a copy in their toolbox to build champions. You will thank me later!"

Antonio L. Crawford, MBA
Director National Christian Writers Conference
Author, Book Coach, Entrepreneur

"*Virtual Reality for Main Street: A Beginner's Guide to Unleashing Our Connections with Virtual Reality*, by Todd Brinkman, is a well written and well researched book. If you are motivated to help others to achieve their dreams, goals and aspirations in a virtual setting, this book is for you! Highly recommended."

Kevin Wayne Johnson
Author, **Leadership with a Servant's Heart: Leading through Personal Relationships**
The Johnson Leadership Group LLC

"A Must Read! The timing of *Virtual Reality for Main Street* to be released to the world is so divinely inspired. Lives will be forever touched, moved, and inspired."

Kim Yeater
Peak Performance Coach

"Virtual reality can be more than a way to play a better video game. *Virtual Reality for Main Street* helped me better understand the possibilities of using VR to support patients in difficult times. This book is an excellent beginner's guide for healthcare professionals interested in learning to embrace technology for good."

Bobbie Battle-Carter, RN, MSN
Founder of Nurse Entrepreneur Academy

"It's time for local chambers to start their innovation conversation. *Virtual Reality for Main Street* is an exciting book as it teaches small businesses to better connect with their prospects and community. I recommend this book as it showcases how easy it is to use VR for the good of your community. This book is a must read for small businesses, places of worship, and healthcare companies."

Rick Wilson
President and CEO
East County Chamber of Commerce

VIRTUAL REALITY

FOR

MAIN STREET

A BEGINNER'S GUIDE TO
UNLEASHING HUMAN CONNECTIONS

TODD BRINKMAN

Virtual Reality for Main Street: A Beginner's Guide to Unleashing Human Connections

Aviva Publishing
Lake Placid, NY
518-523-1320
www.avivapubs.com

Address all inquiries to:
Todd Brinkman
info@vrformainstreet.com
www.vrformainstreet.com

Every attempt has been made to source all quotes properly.

Editors: Tyler Tichelaar and Larry Alexander, Superior Book Productions
Cover Design: Kerry Jesberger, Aero Gallerie
Photographer: Stephanie Jarin @ Jarin Photography
Formatting & Interior Layout: Daniel Hagadorn

Cataloging-in-Publication Data is on file at the Library of Congress
ISBN: 978-1-944335-27-4

10 9 8 7 6 5 4 3 2 1

First Edition, 2020

Printed in United States of America

To the big dreamers who need a
story of hope to persevere.

Contents

Introduction

Embrace Technology to Unleash Your Ability to Connect

Are you ready to help your loved ones thrive in the era of artificial intelligence, quantum computers, robotics, and driverless cars? Then this book is for you. In the following pages, you will learn how to embrace a new tool of our next era to unleash your loved one's ability to connect with others and their community. With virtual reality, you can look to unlock your loved one's capacity to feel connected, loved, and empowered to thrive in our upcoming era.

What if you could virtually bring your parent in assisted living to your holiday dinner? What if you could bring your sibling back to their own past to relive an old memory to remind them they are an overcomer? What if you could bring a friend to the future to celebrate their five-year sobriety celebration? This book shows you how to make these immersive experiences a reality for your family and the people in your community. As you will soon learn, we are now entering a new industrial era that will allow us to connect with each other in ways previously unimaginable.

I'm excited to start this journey with you as we embark into our new industrial revolution. I started this project four years ago to answer one question:

> Virtual reality is coming into our world. How can I help it come into our world for the good of all of us?

Why Read This Book?

In reading this book, you will find that this book is not about you. As I've learned to heal from my wounds, I have started to turn my attention to helping others feel connected, driven, and loved. As you learn to embrace the ideas in this book, my hope is that you begin to turn your attention toward your family members, friends, others in your community, and even your customers. In these efforts, you can look to share the big and everyday experiences together. After completing this book, you will have learned that we don't need to be in the same physical place anymore to feel deeply connected.

Connection Conundrum

I started this journey to understand human connection. In this endeavor, I started conversations with hundreds of other people. I quickly realized I wasn't alone in my feelings of being numb and depressed. I found out that most of us live with the same deep wounds of feeling disconnected. I found it interesting that we have made so many advancements in how we communicate, yet so many of us feel detached and isolated. I found the following statistics alarming:

Suicide In America

- Live Science presented the statistics from the Centers for Disease Control and Prevention (CDC) that rates of death by suicide in the United States have risen by roughly 25 percent in the last couple of decades.[1]

---

1 Erik Vance, June 09, 2018, LiveScience.com, https://www.livescience.com/62781-why-are-suicide-rates-rising.

- NPR recently reported that "Suicide rates have increased in nearly every state over the past two decades, and half of the states have seen suicide rates go up more than 30 percent."[2]

Millennials Depression

- A recent Blue Cross Blue Shield report shows a 47 percent increase in major depression diagnoses with millennials since 2013. More striking is that 20 percent of them are not seeking treatment.[3]
- Depression diagnoses rose 33 percent in America from 2013 to 2016. Up 47 percent among millennials.[4]

Then it dawned on me that we live in a world where, as technology increases, our ability to deeply connect with others decreases. I have learned to understand this phenomenon as our connection conundrum.

This book project just woke me up to the world around me. Our connection conundrum is real! This book's intention is to start a conversation about what is possible in solving this problem of disconnection by helping others become connected and empowered.

Think of the people in your life. What if you could help them feel more deeply connected to their family members, friends, and with their community? What is that worth? Is the idea of this worth a few hours of your time to explore?

---

2 https://www.npr.org/sections/health-shots/2018/06/07/617897261/cdc-u-s-suicide-rates-haveclimbed-dramatically
3 Hillary Hoffower and Allana Akhtar, Oct 10, 2019, https://www.businessinsider.com/millennials-mental-health-burnout-lonely-depressed-money-stress
4 https://www.forbes.com/sites/brucelee/2018/05/12/depression-diagnoses-up-33-up-47-among-millennials-why-there-is-an-upside/#23cd6eeb5061

If you feel it is, I am excited to take you on a journey that will help you connect in ways unimaginable before starting this book. This is a book of possibilities.

Four Types Of Readers

I wrote this book specifically to target four types of readers:

1. Support for your loved ones. I wrote this book to help you connect with your family members and friends from around the world. You will learn to send them an immersive bridge to share in a joyful experience, to feel supported in difficult times, and to create emotionally charged virtual reality dream boards from their future.

2. Support for the people in your community. Support others in your community by creating personal and community experiences. Here, they can take a virtual trip to visit a loved one for a birthday, meditate on the beach, or pray from their place of worship before an upcoming surgery.

3. Healthcare and senior/assisted living executives. As a leader in your community, you can embrace the contents in this book and look at new ways to potentially improve your patient/resident satisfaction surveys, improve key performance indicators (KPIs), empower your staff, and create a legacy of powerfully positive memories between patients/residents and their loved ones.

4. Business leaders. As a business leader, you can look at cutting through the marketing clutter by creating messages that deeply connect with your customers and prospects. With virtual reality, you have a new tool that allows you to deliver "empathic" messaging that can potentially raise conversion rates and other KPIs for a much higher ROI (return on investment).

As you will learn, virtual reality allows your customers/prospects to feel like they are a part of your messaging. In other words, they will feel like they are in the middle of your story, as opposed to a traditional message where they are watching the message as an "outsider."

Book Breakdown

I constructed this book in an easy-to-follow manner that will also be easy to reference in the future. It consists of four parts. It is geared toward demystifying virtual reality by showing you how easy it is to create your own personal and community immersive experiences. This book will help you start a conversation with your family and community about our new realities.

PART ONE. In Part One, we'll take an in-depth look at our new era and the four new realities that will become part of our daily lives. These new realities include augmented, virtual, mixed, and holograms. In this book, we will focus on virtual reality.

PART TWO. Part Two teaches you the two main building blocks of this book.

1. **360 Personal Experiences.** First, you will learn how to create your own 360 personal experiences. This experience will allow you to virtually bring your loved ones to you in the present, to their past, and to their own future. Moreover, you can connect the people in your community with their loved ones for the same purpose. These topics are covered in *Chapters 3-7*.
2. **360 Community Experiences.** Second, you will learn to create 360 community experiences that will allow your loved ones and others in your community to virtually travel to pray from their place of worship, mediate at a local beach, hear an encouraging message, or take a local adventure.

This topic will be covered in *Chapter 8*.

PART THREE. In Part Three, we take what you learned from Part Two to create virtual reality departments. In this part, we switch gears so you can learn how a healthcare or assisted living center executive can embrace virtual reality to help their patients/residents virtually leave where they are and feel like they are somewhere else. This part looks at three local businesses/nonprofits near you.

1. Hospitals in *Chapter 10*.
2. Hospices in *Chapter 11*.
3. Senior/Assisted Living in *Chapter 12*.

PART FOUR. In Part Four, you will learn how to utilize 360 personal and community experiences to form deep connections in your public relations and advertising campaigns. As you will learn, 360 personal and community experiences allow you to bring your target audiences into your story. They will feel a part of your messaging because they will feel like they are with the actors in your 360 video.

Our next industrial revolution is arriving. Let's bring our new tools into our world for the good of us all. Visit **www.vrformainstreet.com** for more information.

I'm looking forward to starting this conversation with you.

Todd Brinkman

Todd Brinkman

PART ONE

What Reality Are You Living In?

Chapter 1
What's Next For Our New Era?

―――――

"Change is the law of life. And those who look only to the past or present are certain to miss the future."

JOHN F. KENNEDY

Our next industrial revolution is upon us. Are you ready to thrive in this new era? If so, then this book is perfect for you. In later chapters, you will learn how to take one of our new tools to radically improve others' ability to feel connected, loved, and empowered. But before we jump in, let's take a step back to see where we are and what is possible in our new era. In this chapter, we will explore:

- **What is next for our world?**
- **What are our new reality tools?**
- **How can we use our new tools for the good of us all?**

What Is Next For Our World?

Quite possibly, this is the first time you have heard that we are now moving into another industrial revolution. The next era in human history is called the Fourth Industrial Revolution. Klaus Schwab described this concept in his groundbreaking book, *Shaping the Fourth Industrial Revolution*.[5]

―――――

5 Schwab, Klaus. *Shaping the Fourth Industrial Revolution*. New York: Penguin, 2018.

Over the next decade, this disruption will fundamentally change the way we work, the way we learn, the way we communicate, and even the way we worship.

Schwab defined this new era in this fashion:

> "The possibilities of billions of people connected by mobile devices, with unprecedented processing power, storage capacity, and access to knowledge, are unlimited. And these possibilities will be multiplied by emerging technology breakthroughs in fields such as artificial intelligence, robotics, the Internet of Things, autonomous vehicles, 3-D printing, nanotechnology, biotechnology, materials science, energy storage, and quantum computing."[6]

What Are Our New Reality Tools?

Another possibility is we will need to learn to live our daily lives with a total of five realities. These new realities will help unlock the idea that we don't need to be physically together to feel a sense of connection. These realities are:

1. **Real reality (reality by itself).**
2. **Augmented reality.**
3. **Virtual reality.**
4. **Mixed reality.**
5. **Holograms.**

1. Real Reality (reality by itself). The real reality is our "traditional" sense of reality with no augmented, virtual, or holographic additions. For example, two people are in the same physical space and engage with each other

----

6 Schwab, Klaus. "The Fourth Industrial Revolution: what it means, how to respond." World Economic Forum. Retrieved 2017-06-29.

engage with each other in a way that does not utilize any additional reality tools.

I've come to define our traditional real reality as:

> The real reality is our traditional reality where we interact with the physical world with no virtual, augmented, or holographic devices.

2. Augmented Reality (AR). Augmented reality is a new reality tool that combines the real reality with a device that overlays digital content. In this new reality, you remain in the real world but can view content that augments what you see. Here are a few examples:

- **Ex. The Resort.** When you check in to a resort, you are handed a pair of augmented reality glasses that help you find your room by projecting an actual green arrow on the floor. That's right. The arrow goes away when you lift your glasses. However, when you put them back on, you see the arrow again. This application could also work with a mobile phone app or another device provided by the resort.

- **Ex. The Mirror.** You can't try on lipstick before you buy it, but what if you could? What if a computer scanned your face and then presented you with an image of yourself on which you could try different colors? That's right; you click ten shades of red, and you get to see what they all look like on your face. No actual lipstick required.

3. Virtual Reality (VR). In preparing for this book, I ran across hundreds of people who had never viewed a virtual reality experience. I enjoyed handing them a virtual reality headset and then helping them watch a 360-degree video of a roller-coaster ride. It was always fun watching their facial expressions when they start up that first incline on their virtual journey and begin to feel nauseous. At the end of the ride, they always react in a way that says, "Wow. What a ride. I felt like I was on the roller coaster."

I bring up a roller coaster specifically to explain the difference between a 360 video and a virtual reality experience. These definitions may sound like splitting hairs, but the differences are worth mentioning.

A full virtual reality experience takes your mind into an immersive environment where you can control your actions with eye movements or by clicking a button on a device. You are free to move around and engage with the experience as you see fit. You are in control of where you go, whom you hang out with, or how you play the game. These will include experiences for business, healthcare, education, spiritual organizations, and personal development. For example:

- **Human Resources:** Simulations that offer the recipient the opportunity to feel engaged and to learn from life like bullying or harassment scenarios.
- **Education:** Educational simulations can teach math, new languages, or how to stop a leak in an oil rig.
- **Relaxation:** Hospital patients can virtually visit a Paris beach to relive their vacations.

360 Video. The roller-coaster ride is an example of a VR simulation. In this scenario, you are watching a recorded video where you can only play, rewind, fast forward, or pause the experience. The remainder of this book will teach you how to create personal 360 videos for your family, friends, and community.

Here is the current Wikipedia definition of virtual reality:

"Currently standard virtual reality systems use either virtual reality headsets or multi-projected environments to generate realistic images, sounds and other sensations that simulate a user's physical presence in a virtual environment."[7]

4. Mixed Reality (MR). Mixed reality headsets allow you to view your real reality with the additional elements of augmented and virtual reality. Here is the definition of mixed reality:

"Mixed reality (MR) is the merging of real and virtual worlds to produce new environments and visualizations where physical and digital objects co-exist and interact in real time. Mixed reality takes place not only in the physical world or the virtual world, but is a hybrid of reality and virtual reality, encompassing both augmented reality and augmented reality via immersive technology."[8]

5. Holograms. At first glance, holograms may seem like a technology years away for us to use in a practical sense. Well, that is not the case. Holographic technology is here and will be entering our daily life within the next few years. In fact, you can currently view President Reagan at his Presidential Library as a hologram.[9] You can watch a Whitney Houston concert with a holographic image of her likeness.[10]

Buckle up. It's right around the corner from our daily life.

---

7 https://en.wikipedia.org/wiki/Virtual_reality
8 https://en.wikipedia.org/wiki/Mixed_reality
9 Chris Woodyard, *USA TODAY*, Oct. 10, 2018
https://www.usatoday.com/story/news/nation/2018/10/10/president-ronald-reagan-3-d-new-hologram-reagan-library/1574147002/
10 Maeve McDermott, *USA TODAY*, Sept. 15, 2015
https://www.usatoday.com/story/life/music/2015/09/15/whitney-houston-hologram-perform-2016/72310440/

How Can We Use Our New Tools For The Good Of Us All?

We will have the option to use these new reality tools for good or bad. We may disagree about the ethics of what's good or bad. But it is important to start this conversation with your family and neighbors. To help support you in this endeavor, the remainder of this book will illustrate how easy it is to create 360 personal and community immersive experiences for the good of us all.

360 Personal Experiences. A 360 personal experience is a 360 video that allows you to virtually bring your loved ones to where you are in the present, to their own past, and even to their own future. This may sound like sci-fi at first. But you will soon learn how easy it is to create and how it will help unleash your ability to stay connected with your loved ones from around the world. Additionally, you will be able to help others connect with their family members and friends.

360 Community Experiences. A 360 community experience is a 360 video that allows people in your area to feel a part of their local community by watching a play at a local community center, relaxing at the beach before surgery, or taking a nature hike from an assisted living facility. It's a 360 video designed for everyone to view in your community or only at a local hospital.

Chapter 1: Summary

Our new era will transform our world through artificial intelligence (AI), quantum computers, robotics, and automation.

This new revolution will be an opportunity to unleash our ability to feel connected, loved, and empowered.

In our new era, we will need to learn how to navigate through our five realities:

1. **The Real Reality.** The real reality is our traditional reality where we interact with the physical world with no virtual, augmented, or holographic devices.
2. **Augmented.** The digital world overlaid with our real world.
3. **Virtual.** Immersive experiences where we feel like we are somewhere else.
4. **Mixed.** Combinations of augmented and virtual experiences.
5. **Holograms.** A 3D image that has a likeness to the person or object.

These new realities will help unlock the idea that we don't need to be physically together to feel a sense of connection.

360 personal experiences virtually bring your family members, friends, people in your community, or your target marketing audience to where you are in the present, to their own past, and even to their own future.

360 community experiences virtually bring your family members, friends, people in your community, or your target audience to a specific place in the present in your community.

Chapter 1: Worksheet

Your First Thoughts

What are you most excited about with virtual reality?

_____

_____

_____

What parts of virtual reality have you concerned?

_____

_____

_____

What ethical and spiritual questions come up for you?

_____

_____

_____

Opportunities

What virtual reality opportunities could support your loved ones?

_____

_____

_____

What virtual reality opportunities do you see that could support your patients?

_____

_____

_____

What virtual reality opportunities do you see that could help you to connect with your customers and prospects?

_____

_____

_____

Chapter 2
Our New Immersive Reality (Virtual Reality)

———

"In virtual reality, we're placing the viewer inside a moment
or a story... made possible by sound and visual
technology that's actually tricking the brain
into believing it's somewhere else."

CHRIS MILK

Does the idea of virtual reality seem abstract? Or do you feel it was only created to play a better video game? If this sounds like you, I wrote this book to help you understand what's possible with one of our new realities called virtual reality. Augmented reality only augments reality; virtual reality completely immerses you in an alternate reality.

As you start an immersive virtual reality experience, you instantly feel like you are walking on Mars, touring the space station, or watching a live sporting event from the field. Virtual reality is not just another video on your phone. It is an immersive experience that virtually brings you somewhere else. It's a virtual trip.

> Virtual reality is not just another video on your phone or TV. It is an immersive experience that virtually brings you somewhere else. It's a virtual trip.

In this chapter, we will take a deep dive into what's possible for our new reality tool in how we work, connect with customers, worship, play, emotionally heal, and travel.

Virtual Reality In Our Daily Lives

Virtual reality is nearly here. Advancements are made every month, and it looks like this new technology will begin to explode upon the arrival of a much faster way to connect to the internet. This faster connection is called 5G. When it arrives, it will have the potential to change our daily lives in six major areas:

1. How We Connect At Work

- **Attend a meeting in virtual reality.** You can now create a live meeting where participants have a 360 view of the conference room. This event gives them the feeling that they are sitting at the conference table with you. In this immersive experience, participants can turn their heads around with their headset. This experience gives them the feeling that they are with you in the room. This meeting concept is radically different from participating via computer or phone.

- **Attend a meeting in virtual reality as an avatar.** An employee can now even enter the meeting as a virtual avatar. This option will allow them to engage with the rest of the staff in the meeting as if they were there in person.

- **Note:** An avatar is a computer-generated character in virtual reality where you share an immersive experience together with others. For example, you can watch a movie on Mars with a sibling. With facial recognition software, you will turn your head with a virtual reality headset on to talk with them in this shared virtual reality experience.

Here, the sibling's avatar will look just like them and engage in ways that mirror real reality. This could change the way we think about what it means to be together. This is the case in this example where two siblings live in different countries but their minds (and hearts) feel like they are together.

- **Construction inspections.** Let's say a construction supervisor is on vacation in Hawaii when something comes up with a project back home. They can instruct a team member to create a live, 360 walking tour video of the property under construction. This live event is radically different from a picture or a video and is much better than having to fly all the way there to view the property.

2. How We Connect With Our Customers

You can now create virtual reality experiences to create deeper connections with your target audience. Your experience will help them view your message in a completely fresh way that will enhance your branding and messaging. We will explore the possibilities of virtual reality in public relations and advertising in Part Four.

- **Public relations.** You can now create empathy for your causes that you support. For example, you can create a virtual reality experience that will showcase the work you do for the homeless in your community. It's not a traditional video on Facebook. This is a fully immersive video that will virtually bring your customers to a homeless shelter where they see your team helping the homeless in your community.

- **Advertising via walking tour.** Bring your customers on a 360 walking tour of your newly remodeled business. A picture or a video is a great idea. But a virtual reality simulation or 360 video takes your advertising message to a whole new level by bringing them into your renovation where they will feel like they are taking a walking tour in person.

3. How We Worship

Later in this book, you'll learn how spiritual organizations can connect members in ways that seemed impossible before virtual reality (and this book). For example, a hospital ministry could virtually bring a hospital patient to their place of worship for prayer.

This immersive video will give the patient the "real" experience of being prayed for as they await or recover from surgery. This experience is not a one-size-fits-all app. This recording is a personal, 360/virtual reality prayer experience. I call this immersive experience a "Virtual Reality Prayer." VR Prayer for short.

4. How We Play

- **Positive aspects of gaming.** Immersive virtual reality gaming is coming to your community. This next generation of gaming allows the gamer to feel like they are in the game. This type of gaming is quite different from playing on a TV screen or a phone. Engaging with this immersive gaming could have many positive attributes.

- **Working with technology.** Gaming can acclimate your family members to using technology to solve problems using a new set of tools. This training could lead to careers in healthcare, the military, and education.

- **Working with others.** Shared virtual reality gaming can bring friends "together" to help solve complex problems and win the game as a team. This team building helps assimilate them to the idea of working with others without being physically in the same place.

- **Empathy.** Research is being conducted on the ability of virtual reality experiences to create empathy for another. I anticipate that video games will deploy this element of socialization.

- **Note:** In Part Three, you will learn how immersive personal experiences allow us to feel empathy toward others. This could allow you to show the plight of the homeless in your community or walk in a loved one's shoes before their surgery (as a secondary recipient). This new reality tool could help us improve the connection conundrum we looked at earlier.

- **Gaming violence.** Many of these games will be extremely violent. This violence may have negative implications on brain development and potentially cause desensitization to violence against others (especially toward women or other races). I'm not here to judge video games because I loved them when I was younger. But it is something to consider.

- **Avatars.** Gamers get to choose their characters. They can be a woman, a man, a werewolf, or even a famous politician. This selection may not be inherently wrong, but I bring it up because your loved ones will have the chance to choose an evil character. With this in mind, a game may allow your loved ones to feel like they are committing criminal acts.

- **Haptics.** This emerging technology employs sensors placed on our bodies that will allow us to engage the virtual environment. If we are punched in the gut in the game, we feel the punch. This physicalness elevates gaming to new levels we do not fully understand yet. A good question to ask would be: What happens when our mind believes (mentally and physically) that we just jumped off a building? Would this have near- and long-term effects?

- **Movies and sports.** You can enjoy a movie or game with family and friends spread out around the globe. This live experience makes it feel like you are there at the cinema/stadium with them.

6. How We Can Support Each Other Emotionally

This book is devoted to covering this topic in detail. My mission is to provide you with the tools to connect with your loved ones in difficult times.

- **360 Personal Experiences.** As you will learn in Part Two, you have three categories of personal experiences.

  - **Current day.** Virtually bring your loved one to your living room for a conversation.
  - **Past.** Bring your parent virtually back to the exact spot of their first kiss with their spouse.
  - **Future.** Take the dream board picture off the wall and turn it into an emotional vision of the possible future for your sibling.

- **360 Community Experiences.** In Chapter 8, you will learn how to create 360 community experiences for the people in your community experiencing difficult times.

  - **Spiritual.** A hospice patient can pray from a local place of worship.
  - **Meditative.** A recovery patient can reflect on their life on a local beach.
  - **Motivational.** A recovery patient can view a local comedian's road to recovery to feel inspired.

- **Adventurous.** A senior in assisted living can feel like they are taking a nature hike.

6. How We Travel

A hotel or resort could bring potential guests on a virtual walking tour of their facility. As the guest places on their headset, they feel like they are by your pool, viewing a VIP room, or exploring your conference rooms. You can create these experiences with 360 cameras or an actual virtual reality environment where they can navigate the experience by themselves.

- **Virtual vacations.** You can learn to take virtual reality trips to your favorite locations. Soon, it may be possible to take a virtual trip for an extended period in a virtual reality application/simulation (not a 360-degree video).

- **Global 360 videos**. Visit YouTube to pick a favorite location to virtually spend time with a 360 video of a mountaintop, national surfing contest, or skydiving jump.

Chapter 2: Summary

Virtual reality will change the way we engage in the workplace because it will look to redefine what a meeting is.

This new reality tool will bring new levels of connection with your public relations and advertising.

Our new era will help shape how we worship and pray for each other.

Our new forms of entertainment will allow us to feel more connected than ever before.

Virtual reality video games may have positive and potentially negative consequences.

Virtual reality may allow us to avoid feeling isolated and disconnected. This will be accomplished by being able to virtually connect with our loved ones and to special places in our local community.

Our new era will allow us to feel like we have taken a virtual trip to another place on Earth or beyond.

Chapter 2: Worksheet

Improve Workplace Culture

How could virtual reality improve your workplace culture?

_____

_____

_____

How could you embrace virtual reality to help remote workers feel connected to your business?

_____

_____

_____

Support For Loved Ones

Fun trip. Where would you virtually bring your parent for an enjoyable trip?

_____

_____

_____

Why?

_____

_____

_____

How would that support them?

_____

_____

_____

Hospital stay. Where would you virtually bring your parent in their stay at a hospital?

_____

_____

_____

Why?

_____

_____

_____

How would that help support them in their stay?

_____

_____

_____

Customers And Prospects

Where would you virtually bring your customers and prospects?

_____

_____

Why?

_____

_____

_____

_____

How would that help you to connect with them?

_____

_____

_____

_____

Community Nonprofits

Which nonprofits in your area would benefit from virtual reality?

_____

_____

_____

What personal experiences would support prison inmates in your community?

_____

_____

_____

What community experiences could you record for local hospital patients to feel encouraged?

_____

_____

_____

PART TWO

Unleash Your Ability To Feel Connected

Chapter 3

What Is A 360 Personal Experience?

"The greatest discovery of all time is that a person can
change his future by merely changing his attitude."

O P R A H   W I N F R E Y

Are you looking for a deeper connection with your long-distance
friends? Have family members moved away and it feels
impossible to stay connected? Would you like to support local
hospital patients to virtually visit their loved ones before
surgery? Chapter 3 will help you better understand how to
create these immersive experiences with your family members,
friends, people in your community, and even your customers.

In Chapter 3, you will learn how to connect with your loved ones
in a way that seemed impossible before this chapter. Here are
the three main points we'll explore:

- **Definition of a 360 personal experience.**
- **Four groups to create a 360 personal experience.**
- **Three types of a 360 personal experience.**

What is a 360 personal experience? It's not about you. Creating a
360 personal experience is not about you, your ambitions, or
even your agendas.

It's about bringing another person to another special place for
encouragement, support, or to feel connected.

Immersive bridge. A personalized immersive bridge is a 360 degree experience that virtually brings a person to a place in the present day, to their own past, or to their own future. This is not a one-size-fits-all application.

As a viewer places on their virtual reality headset, they will be virtually transported to a place that is important to them.

Definition Of A 360 Personal Experience

> A 360 personal experience is a live or recorded immersive personal experience that brings a person virtually someplace in the present, to their own past, or to their future.

Four Groups To Create A 360 Personal Experience

A 360 personal experience can be created by four groups of people in your community. Each of these topics will be covered in detail throughout the book.

1. Your family members and friends. A 360 personal experience allows you to create a 360 video that connects you with your family members and friends. This immersive bridge will help you share experiences that will make you feel like you are together from a world apart.

2. People in your community. Support the people in your community by virtually bringing them to their loved ones throughout the world and to their favorite places in the community. For example, a senior in assisted living can feel like they are having dinner with their sibling who lives across the country. This will be the focus of Part Three.

3. Your team members. As a leader in our new era, you can help your team members take that dream board off their wall and turn it into an inspirational virtual reality dream board from their own future. I will cover this topic in more detail in Chapter 7.

4. Customers and prospects. In Part Four, you will learn how to create 360 personal experiences to deeply connect with your customers and prospects through public relations and advertising messaging.

Three Types Of A 360 Personal Experience

Three types of experiences can be used to connect with your family and friends from a whole world away.

1. Present-day experiences. Present-day experiences allow you to virtually bring others to an important place in the present. Let's look at two examples to help you start wrapping your head around this reality tool.

> A 360 present-day experience allow its viewer to virtually feel like there are somewhere else in that moment in time.

2. Open-chair dinner theme. Your mother is feeling isolated and would like to join you for dinner tonight. However, this is impossible since she lives in an assisted living center in Utah. You now live in Madison, Wisconsin, and it breaks your heart that this simple connection is unlikely. Well, that is until now.

3. One more trip around the lake. Your best friend is in hospice care and unable to travel outside their room. In their last days, you ask them where they would like to go if they could go anywhere. Without hesitation, they say they would like to take one more trip around the lake back in Minnesota.

You jump into action and help to create an immersive bridge where they are on a boat traveling around their favorite lake. It's not sci-fi. This event is a 360 personal experience.

Past Experiences

A customized 360 personal experience allows you to step on the accelerator to go back in time. In these 360 videos, you can support loved ones or a person in your community by creating an experience where they can relive an old memory. Here are two examples to help illustrate what is possible.

> A 360 past personal experience will allow its viewer to step on the accelerator to go back in time to relive old memories.

Father's surgery. Your friend's father is going into surgery. He is distraught with emotional pain because his wife is not with him at this time of great sorrow. She passed away five years ago. You jump into action and gather his family around the exact place where he proposed to her fifty years ago. This experience brings him back to his past to reflect on the fact that he's not alone and he has had a life of great love. This sense of peace could dramatically change the emotional and even physical pain he had before watching this experience.

Fifth anniversary. On your fifth anniversary, you decide to mark the occasion by creating an immersive bridge back to the exact place of your first kiss. On your anniversary night, you place a headset on your wife's head. At this moment, she is virtually transported to that exact spot of your kiss.

I've come to appreciate these personal experiences as being greeting cards to the past.

Future Experiences

In these experiences, you'll also be able to help create immersive bridges to another's own projected future. In these 360 videos, they can start to believe they can achieve their dreams, stay sober, finally lose their weight, or assist in their emotional healing from a car accident. Here are three examples to point you in the right direction.

> A 360 future personal experience allows its viewer to feel like they are living in an experience from their own projected future.

Recovery. Your friend has confided in you that her recovery is going well, but she needs support to remain sober. To accomplish this, you gather her friends, family, and women's group to create a 360 video. You all pretend you are celebrating her sobriety five years in the future. Once completed, she feels immersed in the experience, which helps her to feel like she is in her own future celebrating her own party.

Note: Always receive the permission of your loved ones medical and professional team before delivering this 360 personal experience.

Dream (vision) boards. Your brother has just started his own business. You can tell he is becoming frustrated because things are not working out as he planned. As you know, his dream with this business is to spend more time with his family. You jump into action and create a 360 Dream Board Experience from two years in the future.

In this 360 video, you take him to the beach where his wife and two kids congratulate him on his success. Here, his family tells him how grateful they are that he fought through the heartaches to build this life where they get to see their dad every day.

As you'll learn in this book, many opportunities exist for you as you embrace this new technology for the good of your family. One of my favorites is how we can bring our loved ones to their own future. You get to take that dream board picture off your loved one's wall and turn it into an emotional, virtual experience from their own future—a future where they have already achieved their goal. We will explore this topic in Chapter 7.

Chapter 3: Summary

A 360 personal experience is a live or recorded immersive personal experience that brings a person virtually to an important place in their own present day, to their own past, or to their own future.

A 360 personal experience is not about you.

You can create 360 personal experiences for the following:

- Family members and friends.
- People in your community during difficult times.
- Team members.
- Customers and prospects.

A 360 personal experience can virtually bring someone to:

- The present to visit family, friends, or their favorite place in the world.
- Their own past to relive an old memory.
- Their own projected future to build faith that they can achieve.

Chapter 3: Worksheet

Present Day Experiences

Support for loved ones. Who in your life could you help to feel more connected, loved, and empowered?

_____

_____

_____

Where could you virtually send them to feel connected, loved, and empowered?

_____

_____

_____

How could that immersive experience support them in a difficult time?

_____

_____

_____

Holiday dinner. Who would you virtually invite to your holiday dinner?

_____

_____

_____

Why them?

_____

_____

_____

How would that support them?

_____

_____

_____

Back In Time Experiences

Where could you virtually bring your spouse back in time to feel loved?

_____

_____

_____

Why there?

_____

_____

_____

How would that support them?

_____

_____

Future Experiences

What future personal experiences could you build for your children?

_____

_____

_____

Where would you virtually bring them?

_____

_____

_____

How would this support them?

_____

_____

_____

Chapter 4
Six Steps To Creating Your Own
360 Personal Experiences

———

"The incredible thing about the technology is that you
feel like you're actually present in another place
with other people."

MARK ZUCKERBERG

Thus far, you have learned what is possible with virtual reality. Our next step is to simplify and demystify this complex topic and help you start creating your own 360 personal experiences. As we have learned, virtual reality is not only about playing a better video game. This reality tool can now take your family members, friends, patients, inmates, the homeless, a customer, and your prospects on a personalized virtual trip. These personalized virtual trips can take the above list to one of three locations:

- An important place in the present day to feel connected.
- To their own past to relive a memory.
- To their own future to build their faith that they can achieve their goal of healing, sobriety, or to hit their next promotion.

In Chapter 4, we will take a deep dive into the two main topics.

- **360 personal experience considerations.**
- **How to create your own 360 personal experiences.**

1. 360 Personal Experience Considerations

Creating your own virtual reality (360 video) experiences is as easy as following six easy steps. As we jump in, let's look at a few considerations.

Be patient. The tools of our new era are new to all of us. I suggest you be patient with yourself, others, and this new technology.

Not a techie book. This book's scope is to start a conversation with you about what is possible. Technology in this field is changing so fast that it's impossible to keep up. As a result, this is not a book to help you with operating your 360 camera, using proper use of lighting, finding top new virtual reality headsets, or editing your videos. I will leave that up to the experts in those individual fields. Visit **www.vrformainstreet.com** to hear from these experts on the technical side of creating a 360 video. In fact, visit the website to contribute your thoughts and recommendations.

Teaching others. As you proceed, it is conceivable your family, friends, and others in your community will look to you to help them form these connections. In doing so, you are not alone in your attempts to teach others. Join our community by visiting **www.vrformainstreet.com**.

2. How To Create Your Own 360 Personal Experiences

Creating your own 360 personal experiences requires the use of a six-step process that concerns, in order:

1. **360 Recipients.**
2. **360 Theme.**
3. **360 Participants.**
4. **360 Environment.**

5. 360 Experiences.
6. Delivery.

1. 360 Recipients. 360 Recipients are the people for whom you create the personalized videos. There are three types of recipients: primary, secondary, and time recipient(s).

Primary recipient(s). The primary recipient is the person(s) who instantly knows the video is for them. Here's the simple definition:

> The primary recipient is the person for whom the video is created.

Secondary recipient(s). You can invite others to view your personalized experiences as well. For example, you can invite your mother to watch a birthday party that was created for your sister. Your mother will watch the video as if she's living the party as her own daughter. When a secondary recipient puts on their headset, they instantly know the video was not intended for them. I like to think of this as "walking in another's shoes."

Here is the definition I have assigned to this recipient:

> A secondary recipient is a person who views the 360 personal experience through the eyes of another. This immersive video gives secondary recipients special access into the lives of others. Ultimately, the video allows them to virtually walk in others' shoes to build empathy and better understand their past, present, and projected future.

Let's now explore these four types of secondary participants.

1. Family and friends. These experiences allow you to invite family and friends to share in the 360 videos you are creating. They get to view the experience from the point of view of the primary recipient(s).

2. Strangers. In public experiences, people with no knowledge of the primary recipient(s) can "walk a mile in their shoes." This will create an element of empathy that the stranger will have for the primary recipient. It's never as good as being there in person, but it is the second-best choice for creating understanding.

Here are only a few possible examples:

- Create a community video that highlights the plight of the homeless in your city. This public video may create a new sense of empathy for the homeless.

- Interview a Haitian villager after an earthquake. This heartbreaking story could be used to raise awareness and money for the village.

3. Medical professionals.

- **Mental health professionals.** A mental health professional may gain exclusive access to their patient's past, present, and even their dreams of the future. By walking in the patient's virtual shoes, a professional may ascertain unique glimpses of the many layers of the patient's personality. This viewing could be used to identify the causes of stress or even to identify abuse.

- **Recovery counselors.** A recovery professional or coach can start to walk in their patients' footsteps and gain access to their lives that may otherwise not be available to them.

- **Caregivers in senior/assisted living.** A caregiver in senior/assisted living can gain exclusive access to the wellbeing of their residents.

- **Memory care.** A memory care professional can create and evaluate 360 personal experiences to a primary recipient's own past. This experience may give a professional special access to their patient's mental wellbeing and allow for experimentation to better understand 360 personal experiences' potential use for patient care.

- **Hospital staff.** A hospital employee could better understand their patients as secondary recipients.

In remote cases, you could spot mental abuse or other negative stressors. This is a primary reason that medical professionals should consider viewing these personal experiences before their patients watch the videos. The videos are about helping the patient get through a difficult time without causing additional emotional pain.

As always, get permission from the primary recipient's medical team and caregivers before delivering your immersive experiences. This is new for all of us, and it must be completed with respect for the primary recipients and their medical teams.

> Always get the permission from your primary recipient's medical team and caregivers before delivering 360 personal experiences.

4. Leaders. A business leader can create a 360 personal dream board experience for their team members from their own future. The leader can take their team member's dream board picture off their cubicle wall and turn it into a 360 personal experience in which they feel they have already won. In this experience, your team member will feel like they have accomplished their financial goal, received their promotion, or moved into their new home.

> By watching this experience as a secondary recipient, the leader will gain special access to their employee's personality and goals in life.

From here, you can start a new conversation about their next steps with your company or organization.

Moreover, if agreeable to your employee, you can allow their coworkers the opportunity to get to know their peers by watching this 360 personal experience. By walking in their coworker's shoes, they may appreciate them more as a human being and be able to work more closely with them in the future.

Time recipients. I can see your face right now. No, this not about time travel. A primary or secondary recipient can view these personal videos later in life to relive an experience from their past. Here's the definition of a time recipient:

> A time recipient is either the primary or secondary recipient who views this experience in the future to watch an event from their own past.

It's the same concept as watching a comedy show a year later—you may laugh at different parts than you did the last time you watched it. The same is true when someone views an immersive bridge into their own past. This video could open the viewer's thoughts to forgiveness, gratitude, and the realization that they were loved.

To get started, let's look at two examples:

- **New baby experience theme.** New parents record a loving experience in which they bring their new child home and say a special prayer for the child's future happiness and wellbeing. The parents store the experience on their computer to show to their child as the child grows older.

  Twelve years later, one of the child's parents is killed in a car accident. In this moment of grief, the remaining parent hands the child a headset. The 360 personal experience virtually takes the child back to the initial homecoming and the prayer the parents offered. As the child watches the immersive bridge to the past, they can reconnect with their absent parent in ways we never thought possible until now.

- **Twentieth anniversary.** A couple is celebrating their tenth wedding anniversary, and one decides to create an experience for the other to view to remind them of how much they are loved. This video brings them back in time to the exact place of their first kiss. In this video, one lovingly tells the other about that day and how it changed their life forever.

  Fast forward ten years, when one spouse has passed away. On their twentieth anniversary, the surviving spouse decides to view this video to remind them of their great love. Donning the headset, they are transported to that exact experience ten years earlier. This connection brings their mind back in time, allowing them to relive an old memory.

Who knows where technology will take us in the future? However, I mention these examples to illustrate that you can view these experiences from different vantage points in time.

2. 360 Theme. The next step is to identify the theme of why you are creating this video. I have learned to call this the 360

Theme. There are an unlimited number of possible themes, but I have broken them into three categories.

> A 360 Theme is the intention of your 360 personal experience.

- **Times of joy (Chapter 5).** In this theme, you can create an experience to connect with your loved ones in times of great joy. This joyful video could be of a new baby, a new job, an engagement, a wedding, or a retirement celebration.

- **Times of difficulty (Chapter 6).** These experiences can help support loved ones in times of significant physical and/or emotional stress. You can now virtually come together to offer support, prayers, and comfort.

- **Times for personal development (Chapter 7).** This type of experience offers your family members, friends, and people in your community the opportunity to view their projected future to believe in themselves. Secondly, a business can help their customers, prospects, and shareholders to feel connected to a project's vision. We will cover this topic extensively in Chapter 7 and in Part Four.

3. 360 Participants. It is imperative to include the best 360 participants available. These participants are the people who will be in the video recording. You may have noticed I don't discuss how to create experiences for yourself.

This book focuses on exploring how to create experiences for your intended primary recipient(s). 360 personal experiences are not about you. They're about creating a personal experience for your family member, friend, patient, inmate, coworker, or employee to watch hundreds of times to build their faith, be encouraged, and even be reminded that they are not alone.

360 Participants are the people in the recording of your 360 personal experience.

- **Wording.** Work with the primary recipient(s) medical and support team to learn how to use the correct wording to be encouraging and supportive. Your experience's goal is to create a positive personal experience that the primary recipient may watch hundreds of times.

- **Surprise 360 participants.** You can choose to create a personal experience that records a surprise cast of family members, friends, and coworkers into your 360 video. Some examples include a surprise birthday or retirement party.

A 360 surprise personal experience is an excellent choice for a surprise party from a distance.

- **Recommended 360 participants.** As the creator of this experience, you may need to ask the primary recipient(s) whom they would like to see in their personal experience.

4. 360 Environment. This step is critical because the environment should be personalized to your primary recipient(s). When the primary recipient puts on their headset, they need to know exactly where they are.

The 360 Environment is the actual place where you are virtually bringing your 360 recipients. This environment can be in the past, present, or future.

Here are a few examples to get you started.

- **Backyard grilling**. It's the Fourth of July, and you create an experience for your family and friends to join you at your lake cabin. When they enter your experience, they feel like they are sitting next to you by the grill.

- **Cancer diagnosis.** Your best friend from church has just found out they have cancer. Without telling your best friend, you gather other friends and head out to your best friend's favorite hiking spot. At the trailhead, you create an experience in which you, your shared friends, the patient's family, and spiritual leader for a positive outcome. In this prayer, everyone lets your best friend know they are not alone. Your best friend will watch this video thousands of times during their treatment.

5. 360 Experiences. The next step is to record your experiences with the 360 camera. Here are a few things to consider in creating your video.

> The 360 Experience is the recording of your 360 personal experience.

- **How the video will be viewed.** You need to decide the primary recipient's position when they are viewing the 360 video. Will they be on a rotating stool, standing, sitting, or lying down? This step is essential because you will need to know whether the viewer can turn around within the experience. Once this is determined, you can record your 360 video in the correct manner.

- **How-to videos.** Due to this book's limited scope, I won't be covering the technical aspects of creating your 360 videos. Please follow your 360 camera's instructions for recording your video.

Visit **www.vrformainstreet.com** for information on top-rated 360 cameras, editing, lighting, discounts, and expert advice.

- **Permissions on private property.** You always need to get permission to record your experience on personal, business, or government property.

- **Permission for copyrighted music or art.** In your recording, make sure you don't intentionally or even unintentionally record background music, art, or anything else that has copyright protection.

- **Permission of participants.** It may be unlawful and impolite to record a participant in your video without that person's permission. Due to the inherent viral nature of your videos, it is conceivable that a public video on social media will be shared and viewed by hundreds of people. Always be polite and ask for permission before recording anyone.

- **Doctor's permission.** In all healthcare-related scenarios, I would suggest getting prior approval from medical professionals before proceeding with any 360 personal experience. The medical team will need to evaluate the primary recipient(s) physical and emotional state to ensure they can watch this immersive experience.

- **Mental health considerations.** Consult with the primary recipient(s) mental health professional due to the potential of unintended effects, such as dizziness, irritation, anger, anxiety, or even depression. This permission is especially needed when virtually bringing your loved ones back to their past. These videos have the potential to bring up painful, negative memories.

- **Healthcare considerations for physical conditions.** The primary recipient's medical team should view and deliver the headset as part of their care. Things to consider may include the patient's mental wellbeing, nausea, level of anesthesia, or dizziness. Other possible adverse reactions may include complications with sound, lights, and flashing lights. In this case, I would have the medical team administer the headset.

- **Hearing impaired.** Many primary recipients will be unable to properly hear your personal experience. In this case, I would add the text of the 360 participants' spoken words. This can easily be accomplished by editing your video. Check with your 360 camera instructions for their recommended editing software.

- **Privacy and security with personal information.** It is imperative that you never disclose your loved one's name, address, hospital, or medical condition in your experiences.

- **Personal property.** It's sad to have to bring this up, but in creating public experiences in your home, you should cover up or hide anything of value.

- **Live vs. recorded.**

  - **Live experiences.** You can create a live experience to bring in support from family and friends on social media.

  - **Recorded experiences.** In most scenarios, I would recommend recording the experience and uploading it to YouTube or Facebook.

- **Public vs. private.**

  - **Public experiences (live).** You have the option of recording a public event for others to watch from the point of view of your primary recipient(s). To create this live experience, connect your 360 camera to your Facebook or YouTube channel, and select the live option. Follow the camera's instructions or visit **www.vrformainstreet.com** for more information.

- **Private experiences (link).** YouTube offers you control over who gets to view your experiences. You can upload your video to YouTube and receive a private link. This private link is the only access to view the 360 video.

Or phone only. You can upload the experience to just your phone for ultimate security.

- **Virtual reality station.** Your hospital, senior living home, or business can create a private place to view your personal experiences. I call this a virtual reality station. This station can be in a quiet room or mobile unit to bring with you out into the community. Here, you can take out the 360 camera's memory card and upload the content directly to the organization's desktop or laptop.

A Virtual Reality Station is a safe and quiet place in a business or home to view 360 personal experiences, 360 community experiences, and VR simulations.

This process will protect the video from being uploaded to social media and to protect your new copyrighted videos. In doing so, you may find it easier to receive permission to record videos of important places in your community because these videos will only be watched in a recovery center or a local hospital (not on Facebook).

- **Duration of 360 video.** You will need to be aware of your duration in recording your videos. I would recommend keeping most recorded videos to ten minutes. This will ensure the video size is not too large to be uploaded to social media and that your 360 camera doesn't overheat. Live experiences can be longer. You will need to experiment for yourself on the best practices for your 360 camera as each camera has different capacities.

- **Editing.** You can edit your 360 videos with a multitude of editing software. This book does not cover editing tips and instructions. Please refer to your camera's instruction manual for best software recommendations. I recommend you hire a local editing specialist in your community to help polish your personal experience.

6. 360 Delivery. The last step is to ensure your primary recipient(s) views the experience correctly. I am assuming your loved ones aren't familiar with properly viewing a 360 video. Therefore, you will need to make it as easy as possible for them.

> A 360 Delivery ensures that your 360 recipients will safely and effectively view your 360 personal experience.

Four types of delivery.

1. Individual, in-person delivery. An in-person delivery allows you to maximize the compassion of the experience. In this delivery, you can personally deliver your care package. This care package could include a headset, a framed picture of the recording, a signed greeting card, and a present.

2. Group in-person delivery. A group delivery is when a group personally delivers the experience. This group could be family, a Scout troop, or a dance class.

3. Medical professional/caregiver assisted delivery. I suggest the doctor, medical team, or caregiver approve the video that will be delivered in a medically supervised setting (i.e., hospital room or assisted living). After its approval, I recommend your primary recipient's medical team administer (put on) the headset. This topic is explored in more detail in Part Three.

- **Prior to delivery.** It may be advisable for a caregiver to discuss this virtual trip beforehand with the primary recipient. In this conversation, the caregiver can discuss how they will feel like they are with family or friends. This may be an emotional experience for the primary recipient.

- **During delivery.** Caregivers may need to monitor the primary recipient to ensure they are safe. Safety in this delivery is essential because the primary recipient may want to walk around, swat things in the air, or reach out to hug a family member.

- **Post delivery.** Caregivers may need to help bring the primary recipients back to the real reality—one with no virtual or augmented realities present.

4. Mailed. In this scenario, the loved one will mail the experience to the primary recipient or to their medical team. A care package would be the right choice here. This package may help personalize the recording.

More importantly, this package ensures they have the correct headset and instructions on how to view your experience.

Types of virtual reality headsets. The following list is a starting point to illustrate the three main types of headsets available. VR Headset pricing, availability, and technology are revised every month.

▪ **1. Value headsets.** Value headsets are between $5 and $20 each. These headsets require you to place your cellphone into the headset to view the virtual reality experience or 360 video. In this book, we will look at utilizing these headsets due to their low cost, ease of use, ability to work with most cellphones, and because we are working with 360 videos only.

To view a 360 video, you simply insert your phone into the headset and watch the video through your YouTube or Facebook app. Here are four quick steps for viewing a video:

- **Step 1: Download the social media application.** Download YouTube (or YouTube VR) or Facebook from your phone's store.

- **Step 2: Find the 360 video.** Find your video on YouTube or Facebook or click on the private link for a private video. Once you have found your video, simply click on the headset icon on the video to view it in virtual reality. You're ready to go when you see a double image of your video.

- **Step 3: Insert phone into headset.** Then simply insert the phone into the headset.

- **Step 4: Place on the headset.** Place on the headset to view the experience. You may also need to attach headphones to better hear the experiences. This will require a minute or two of trial and error.

▪ **2. Mid-range headsets (phone required).** The next set of headsets jump up to the $100 to $200 range. These headsets allow you to watch virtual reality experiences in a standalone device that is not connected to a computer and only requires your cellphone to be inserted.

With this type of headset, you can watch 360 videos, but now you can also watch full virtual reality experiences in applications such as Samsung VR and Oculus. With these applications, you can participate in advanced virtual reality games, watch a movie on the moon, or learn about our solar system.

No phone (or cords) required. These standalone headsets do not require a phone or a connection to your computer. This headset is currently $199.

- **3. High-end headsets.** The last level of headsets is the top of the line. This caliber of headsets does not require your cellphone because it is attached to your gaming computer through a special cord. These headsets range from $300 to $500.

Virtual reality stations. As we learned earlier, creating a virtual reality station would be the best choice to deliver your 360 personal experiences in a professional setting. Primary recipients would simply access their 360 personal experience by plugging their own headset into the computer. The video's quality will be much greater when you watch the video from your computer. Your 360 personal experience loses much of its quality in the download from Facebook and YouTube. I would suggest only using a high-end headset for your virtual reality station.

Chapter 4: Summary

A 360 personal experience will affect three types of people: primary recipient(s), secondary recipient(s), and time recipient(s).

The primary recipient is the person for whom the video is created.

A secondary recipient is a person who views the 360 Family Experience through the eyes of another. This immersive video gives secondary recipients special access into the lives of the primary recipient(s).

Ultimately, the video allows the secondary recipient to virtually walk in others' shoes to build empathy and better understand their past, present, and projected future.

Secondary recipients include family members, friends, strangers, medical professionals, and leaders.

A time recipient is either the primary or secondary recipient who views this experience in the future to watch an event from their own past.

The 360 theme is the reason or purpose for which you are creating your video.

The 360 participants are the people in your recording.

The 360 environment is a special place that is personally important to the primary recipient.

This 360 Experience is the moment when you record your experience with a 360 camera.

Always receive permission from where you are recording, any copyrighted materials, the 360 participants, and the primary recipient's medical team.

Your experiences can either be public (social media) or private (private links, phone only, or virtual reality station).

Your experience can be recorded live or as a recording.

There are four ways to deliver your experience:

1. Individual in-person.
2. Group in-person.
3. Medically assisted.
4. Mailed.

There are three types of headsets:

1. Value headsets.
2. Mid-range headsets.
3. High-end headsets.

Chapter 4: Worksheet

Now it's your turn. The next few pages will allow you to construct your own 360 personal experience. In this example, you will be creating an experience to encourage your sibling in difficult time.

360 Recipients

- **Primary Recipient:** Your primary recipient will be your sibling.
- **Secondary Recipients:** Family and friends.

Which family members and friends will be watching this video as secondary recipients?

_____

_____

Public experience. In a public experience, how will your secondary recipients, who are strangers, be emotionally moved by your 360 video to create empathy with your sibling.

_____

_____

_____

What words would you have the 360 participants say to resonate with these strangers?

_____

_____

_____

360 Themes

Your theme will be to encourage your sibling in a difficult time. Write down your favorite theme idea.

_____

_____

_____

How would this theme help them to feel encouraged?

_____

_____

_____

360 Participants

Who should be in the immersive video recording?

_____

_____

_____

What would they say to encourage your sibling?

_____

_____

_____

360 Environment

Where would you like to virtually bring your sibling in the present?

_____

_____

_____

Where could you bring them to their past?

_____

_____

_____

Where could you virtually bring them in their future to build their faith?

_____

_____

_____

360 Experience

What is your budget to create an experience?

_____

_____

_____

_____

What is your background in creating videos?

_____

_____

What do you need to learn?

_____

_____

_____

What permissions will you need to record and deliver your immersive experience?

_____

_____

_____

Will this be a live or recorded video?

_____

Will this be a private or public video?

_____

360 Delivery

How will you deliver your 360 personal experience?

_____

_____

_____

Will the primary recipient be standing, rotating in a stool, sitting, or lying down?

_____

_____

_____

Will you be delivering your personal experience in person or by mail?

_____

_____

_____

What will you include in your care package?

_____

_____

_____

Chapter 5
Create 360 Personal Experiences For Joy

"VR is a way to escape the real world into something
more fantastic. It has the potential to be the
most social technology of all time."

PALMER LUCKEY

Do you wish you could share more of your life's joyful moments with your family and friends? What life events would you share? This chapter explores this question for you. In this chapter, you will learn how to virtually invite your family and friends to where you are as you are experiencing joyful times. In reverse, you could teach your family and friends to create a joyful experience for you to virtually visit. As you become skilled in these videos, you may look at supporting others in creating connections with their loved ones.

Chapter 5 is devoted to sharing five easy-to-follow examples that will show you what's possible with our new reality tool. In this chapter, we will explore 360 personal experiences that connect primary recipients to an important place in the present, to relive a memory from their past, or to watch their future goal be achieved.

Learn From A Story Examples

I broke this chapter up into four categories that will allow you to reference them later or to share with others how to create their own joyful personal experiences. These examples are presented in a story format to help you clarify how to create your own.

1. **Present Day Common Events.**
2. **Present Day Big Life Events.**
3. **Back To The Past.**
4. **Forward In Time.**

1. Present Day Common Events. In our lives, we can take the simplest things for granted. For example, even a simple Sunday night dinner can create a positive experience when family members can't physically be together. It's not designed to replace being together in person. But you can create this simple 360 personal experience to help connect people in ways that seemed unimaginable before reading the following chapter. In this endeavor, you can look to support your loved ones and the people in your community.

- **Your loved ones.** In normal everyday experiences, you can send family members and friends an immersive bridge to join you for dinner tonight, open the Christmas presents under the tree, or sit on the deck on the lake. I will present two examples to help illustrate how you can quickly create your own.
  - Sunday Dinner
  - Christmas Dinner

- **People in your community.** Personal experiences allow the people you are responsible for to virtually join their loved ones during common events in their lives. Here are four possibilities to create a joyful personal experience in your community.
  - A hospital patient can open Christmas presents with their grandchildren.
  - A hospice patient can once more stroll around their favorite lake.

- A senior in assisted living can feel like they are at their sister's birthday party.
- A homeless person can hear an inspirational message from a local spiritual leader at a shelter.

- **Open-chair Sunday dinner experience**. We tend to appreciate even the simplest things like a family dinner. In the first example, let's take a journey with a family member who lives in a different country and would like to enjoy a simple dinner with their family from a world away.

  After creating your own videos, you can duplicate this experience for others in your community.

> A 360 Personal Experience allows you to share even the most common family events.

Backstory. Your sibling has recently moved to San Diego and misses Sunday night dinners back in Mexico City. You decide to send out an immersive bridge so they can join your family for Sunday night dinner.

360 Recipients

- **Primary Recipient:** Sibling who lives in San Diego.
- **Secondary Recipients:** None.

360 Theme

- An ordinary Sunday dinner.

360 Participants

- Family and friends in Mexico City.

360 Environment

- The kitchen table.

360 Experience

- **Point of view.** Your sibling enters the dining experience as if they were sitting at the table. They will be seated between you and your mother.

- **Setup.** You place your new 360 camera on a small tripod. Next, you set the tripod on an open chair between you and your mother and raise it to eye level. That's it. It's that simple.

- **Note:** Your 360 videos should be recorded at eye level because your primary recipient will enter your immersive experience as if they are sitting/standing next to you. This will give the primary recipient the feeling that they are sitting at the table with the 360 participants (people at the table).

- **Recording.** You count down from three and then press start on the phone app that controls the 360 camera. At this point, your mother starts with a funny message for everyone. Afterward, you have your traditional family dinner. The total video recording lasts ten minutes.

- **Note:** Follow your 360 camera instructions on how to connect your phone and 360 camera.

- **Uploading.** Next, upload your video in four steps:

  1. Upload the video from your camera to your phone.
  2. Create a YouTube channel.
  3. Upload the video from your phone to your YouTube Channel as a private video.
  4. Capture the private YouTube link.

360 Delivery

- **Mailing.** Later that evening, you prepare a care package that you'll send to your sibling. In the care package, you have included a virtual reality headset, instructions on how to view the experience, the private YouTube link, a framed picture of everyone at the table, and a "We miss you" card.

- **Note:** The main reason to mail a care package is to ensure that the primary recipient(s) has a proper virtual reality headset and instructions on how to view your immersive bridge.

- **Viewing.** A few days later, your sibling receives the package via FedEx. They quickly learn how to view the experience and place on the headset. Starting playback, your sibling feels like they are back home in Mexico City. They know it's not the same as being there in person, but it feels so close to reality.

- **Open-chair Christmas memories.** Invite family and friends to join you for Christmas this year. They may live around the country, but they can feel like they are joining you at the kitchen table. During this time, your virtual guests could share in your fun Christmas memories. Additionally, whom could you help in your community with a personal connection like this during the holidays?

Backstory. Christmas is next month, and you would love to invite family and friends to Christmas dinner. Everyone is now scattered around the country, but that doesn't have to stop you anymore.

360 Recipients

- **Primary Recipients:** You have decided to invite your sibling and your older child in college.

- **Secondary Recipients:** None.

360 Theme

- An open-chair Christmas dinner experience.

360 Participants

- The regular Christmas crew.

360 Environment

- Your kitchen table on Christmas night.

360 Experience

- **Point of view.** Your loved ones enter your dinner experience as if they were sitting at your table.

- **Setup.** Place your 360 camera on a tripod and raise it to eye level on an open chair at your table. That's it. It's that simple to get started.

- **Recording.** Everything is set up and ready to go. You press start on the phone app to begin recording. You welcome everyone joining virtually, and you briefly share how much you miss everyone. You proceed to create a ten-minute video of everyone simply enjoying dinner together.

- **Uploading.** After the video's completion (and dinner), you proceed to create a private link for your virtual guests to use:

  1. Uploading the video to your phone.
  2. Uploading it to your YouTube channel as a private video.
  3. Getting the private YouTube link to send out.

4. Once you have the link, you can send it to your virtual guests so they can view your recorded invite-only event on YouTube.

360 Delivery

- **Mailing.** Three weeks before the recording, you send your primary recipients a package that includes a headset, instructions on how to view the experience, and your Christmas present. You will send the private link on Christmas Day after your recording.

- **Viewing.** At their homes, your guests don their headsets to join you for Christmas dinner. Your virtual guests will watch this video many times throughout the year to feel that connection.

2. Present Day Big Life Events. Our life's big events are things we will always remember. With a 360 personal experience, you can send an immersive bridge to a loved one to have them feel like they are at your wedding reception or to help an inmate reconnect with their dying father. I think of these as joyful times because technology can now connect us in ways that weren't available to us until now. Some of these experiences will be light, some will be funny, and some will be the most important memories we have.

Life is supposed to be shared with our loved ones, and we don't have to be in the same physical place to feel connected any longer. Here are two examples I will walk you through in learning how to create a present-day big life event experience.

- Graduation party.
- New home tour.

Invite your grandparent to your graduation. We often wish to show gratitude to or celebrate with family and friends who can't be with us in person. We are no longer bound by physical boundaries to share an experience. In this example, we will learn how to share our special days with loved ones around the world.

Backstory. Your big graduation day is here! You're finally graduating from high school. As the date approaches, you sincerely wish your grandparent could make it to your party. However, they moved back to Poland three years ago and cannot attend. After careful reflection, you begin to create an immersive bridge so they can join you on this big day. You know that this 360 video would be a great surprise.

360 Recipient

- **Primary Recipient:** Your grandparent.
- **Secondary Recipitent:** None.

360 Theme

- Fun theme of gratitude.

360 Participants

- Only you.

360 Environment

- The backyard at your graduation party.

360 Experience

- **Point of view.** Walking around in your backyard.

- **Setup.** You place the 360 camera on your selfie stick and set the camera at eye level as you stretch out your arm as far as you can. When the selfie stick is at eye level, you are ready to get started.

- **Note:** Another way to accomplish this video is by placing your 360 camera on a friend's helmet as they walk next to you during your tour. In this scenario, the person talking will need to look into the 360 camera as if it were the primary recipient(s).

- **Recording.** When you are ready, press start on your phone app and begin to take your grandparent on a walking tour of the yard. During this tour, you can thank them for everything they've done for you and provide details of the big day.

- **Uploading.** After the ten-minute recording, upload it to your YouTube Channel. This will be a private message so you will need to get the private link from YouTube.

360 Delivery

- **Mailing.** The next day, you send a care package that includes a headset, a framed picture of the graduation, instructions on how to view the experience, and a thank you card.

- **Viewing.** Once your grandparent receives the package, they will call you to learn how to view your 360 video. As they put on the headset, they will virtually travel to your backyard on your special day. You know your grandparent will watch this a hundred times to stay connected to you in ways they didn't think were possible.

New home tour. Embrace virtual reality by bringing your family and friends on a tour of your new home. They may live around the country, but they will enjoy the experience of connecting with you during your big life event.

Creating a video on your phone is a great choice. But why not bring them on a virtual tour instead?

Backstory. You and your family are so excited that you have just purchased your new home. You've waited years for this moment and would like to share a live tour with your family and friends.

360 Recipients

- **Primary Recipients:** You invite your parents, your in-laws, and an old friend.
- **Secondary Recipients:** Other friends and family watch on your Facebook page.

360 Participants

- You, your spouse, your two children, and your dog.

360 Environment

- A walking tour of your new home.

- **Note:** You should consider hiding valuables from a public Facebook video.

360 Experience

- **Point of view.** Your virtual guests will feel like they are in your house taking a tour.

- **Setup.** Place the 360 camera on your selfie stick and extend the stick out at arm's length and eye level.

- **Recording.** When you're ready, start the live recording on Facebook and the tour around the house.

You will talk to the 360 camera as if you were making eye contact with your guests.

- **Uploading.** The upload will occur in real time on your Facebook page.

- **Note:** Follow your 360 camera's instructions on how to create a live Facebook event. Make sure your 360 camera can create live Facebook posts before you make your camera purchase.

360 Delivery

- **Store pickup.** No mailing. Everyone will need to purchase their own virtual reality headsets at a local retail store.

- **Note:** Value headsets cost between $5 and $20 at a big box retail store near you.

- **Viewing.** Your Facebook friends will watch the event by donning their headsets as your experience unfolds.

- **Note:** Your Facebook friends will not need a headset to watch the experience. They can simply move their finger (phone) or mouse (computer) to turn the 360 video around to experience the 360 content.

3. Back To The Past. Next, virtual reality allows you to step on the gas pedal going back in time. You can now virtually bring your loved ones, hospital patients, hospice patients, your employee, or a senior in assisted living back to their own past to relive an old memory.

We will expand on this topic as you move through the book. But let's look at one example so you will better understand what's possible.

New engagement. Your friend is getting married. You are so excited, but you quickly realize you can't be there for her in person to share in this special time. With a 360 personal experience, you can now bring your newly engaged friend an immersive bridge to virtually bring her to a special place from her past. After reading this example, you never have to say "Wish you were here" ever again.

Backstory. Your best friend announces their engagement on Facebook. You can't be there in person to congratulate them since they moved away three years ago. You jump into action to bring your friend back to the most memorable place of your group's childhood. You think to yourself; a card just won't cut it. This announcement is such a big thing that you decide to send a 360 greeting card (a 360 personal experience).

360 Recipients

- **Primary Recipient:** Your best friend.
- **Secondary Recipients:** Friends and family who will watch the experience live on your Facebook page.

360 Theme

- A funny video that brings your best friend back to the cabin you hung out at as kids.

360 Participants

- You gather the other two members of your childhood group from back in the day.

360 Environment

- Without hesitation, you decide the video has to be shot at the end of the dock at your parents' cabin.

360 Experience

- **Point of view.** This experience will bring your best friend right to the end of the dock.

- **Setup.** Place your 360 camera on a tripod and raise it to eye level near the end of the dock.

- **Recording.** When you're ready, you and your friends surround the camera. At this point, on your phone, you select a live option on Facebook and then press start to create your live feed. Next, you begin to remind your best friend (and everyone on Facebook) of all the funny things you did as kids. Additionally, you thank them for being such a good friend and tell their new fiancé(e) how very lucky they are.

- **Uploading.** You are live streaming, so the upload is ongoing during filming.

360 Delivery

- **Store pickup.** Before the experience, you ask your newly engaged friend to grab a headset and watch your Facebook page for a surprise on Sunday at 10:00AM. Your friend has told you they already know how to use their headset.

- **Viewing.** As your newly engaged friend puts on their headset, they instantly recognize where they are and remember their old friends. What a special engagement gift!

4. Forward In Time. The possibility of a 360 personal experience allows you to bring your loved ones, patients, team members, or the homeless to their own futures to build faith that they can achieve their goals. We will cover this topic extensively in Chapter 7. Here are a few themes to help you get started:

- **Sobriety:** Virtually bring a recovery patient to their five-year sobriety celebration.

- **Team members:** Virtually bring your star employee to their own future where they are receiving their promotion three years in the future.

- **Homeless:** A homeless shelter can create a personalized celebration from the future for a homeless person where they are living in their own home again.

- **Patient recovery:** Run a real 5k with your friend who is in traction after an accident.

Chapter 5: Summary

You have learned how to create present day common events for your family members, friends, and people in your community.

You now have the tools to create an experience that goes back in time or into the future.

Chapter 5: Worksheet

Let's jump into action and learn to create your own 360 joyful personal experience. Here are some questions to get you started.

360 Recipients

Who is your primary recipient(s)?

_____

_____

Who will be your secondary recipient(s)?

_____

_____

360 Theme

What is the purpose of your personal experience?

_____

_____

_____

How will this support the primary recipient(s)?

_____

_____

_____

360 Participants

Who will be in your video (360 participants)?

_____

_____

_____

Why did you choose them?

_____

_____

_____

What will they say in your recording?

_____

_____

_____

360 Environment

Where are you virtually bringing your primary recipient(s)?

_____

_____

_____

Are you virtually bringing the primary recipient to their present, past, or their future?

_____

_____

_____

Why there?

_____

_____

How will this environment support them?

_____

_____

_____

360 Experience

How will you record and upload your video (360 experience)?

_____

_____

_____

What permissions will you need?

_____

_____

_____

Will the experience be live or recorded?

_____

_____

_____

Will your experience by public on social media? Or private?

_____

_____

_____

360 Delivery

Will you deliver your 360 video in person or mail it?

_____

_____

_____

What would you include in the care package?

_____

_____

_____

Chapter 6

Create 360 Personal Experiences
For Difficult Times

———

"Virtual reality is a technology that could actually allow you to connect on a real human level, soul-to-soul, regardless of where you are in the world."

C H R I S   M I L K

Life throws us curve balls throughout our lives. During these times, you can create 360 personal experiences to bring loved ones and people in your community virtually somewhere else to feel connected with family members, friends, and with other places that are important to them. These personal experiences in difficult times may be the most memorable memories of a primary recipient's life. In these darker times, they will be reminded that they are not alone and are loved.

Always get the permission of your loved one's medical team before delivering a 360 personal experience.

Chapter Examples

I have created four types of examples to help clarify how to support others in difficult times. These 360 personal experiences are for recovery, encouragement, tragedy, and grieving.

1. Recovery. Learn how to create a supportive personal experience in times of recovery from addiction or an accident. A person's body may be in a place of recovery, but their mind (and heart) can take a virtual trip to spend time with their loved ones or to a special place. We will explore three examples:

- Forgiveness after a DUI.
- Can't make dance class after an accident.
- Encouragement after a car accident.

2. Encouragement. Many times, our loved ones, patients, and the homeless feel alone and isolated. In these times, you can send an immersive bridge to connect them with the important people in their lives. We will look at two examples of encouragement:

- Encouragement from a recent job loss.
- Support from a recent divorce.

3. Community Tragedy. Learn how to create a 360 personal experience during a community tragedy.

4. Grieving. The last example will review how you can support a grieving friend

1. Recovery Examples

Here are three examples to showcase what's possible in supporting a loved one or person in your community during times of recovery.

1. Open chair forgiveness after DUI. First, let's look at how you can create a personal experience for forgiveness.

Backstory. A person in your community has admitted they have a drinking problem and has a heart-to-heart with their new sobriety coach. This conversation lays the groundwork to start healing their heart. This 360 video will illustrate that this person is not in this fight of sobriety by themselves. Their sobriety coach jumps into action to create an experience that will help them believe a life of sobriety is possible.

360 Recipients

- **Primary Recipient:** A person in your community who is looking to become sober.
- **Secondary Recipient:** None. Private experience.

360 Theme

- Forgiveness and a hope for sobriety.

360 Participants

- You (their sobriety coach) organize an event with the recovering person's loved ones.

360 Environment

- Childhood home of the person starting their recovery (ten miles away).

360 Experience

- **Point of view.** The person in recovery will enter the experience as if they are standing in the backyard where they grew up.

- **Setup.** As the sobriety coach, you gather the participants in the backyard. You place the 360 camera on a tripod, place it on one of the chairs, and raise the tripod to eye level. You have everyone sit down and surround the 360 camera. That's it. You are ready to begin your experience.

- **Recording.** At this point, you begin by pressing "record" on your phone. As the ten-minute recording starts, the participants get to describe how much they care about their loved one and that they support their loved one's goal of sobriety.

- **Uploading.** This video only gets uploaded to your phone due to its private contents.

- **Note:** Uploading an experience only to your phone is a best practice to keep the 360 video private.

360 Delivery

- **Personal delivery.** After recording the message, you quickly upload the video to your phone and drive over to the recovering person's home. You hand them a care package that includes a framed picture of the participants, a celebration card, viewing instructions, and a headset. You quickly get the event ready on your phone, slide the phone into the headset, and then press play.

- **Viewing.** The person in recovery becomes immersed in an experience from earlier that day. They will watch this personal experience thousands of times to remind them that their new life of sobriety is possible, and they are not alone.

2. Dancing with the Stars. As we age, it's funny what we remember, isn't it? Creating a 360 personal experience can be transformative and help reinforce positive life lessons.

Backstory. Your child's friend in dance class recently broke an arm and can't attend dance class for a couple of months. All the kids in the class begin to miss them and would like to do something special.

You jump to action by calling the child's mother and asking for permission to create an experience to brighten the child's day.

360 Recipients

- **Primary Recipient:** Your child's friend who is in a cast.
- **Secondary Recipients:** None.

360 Participants

- The instructor and all the kids in the dance class.

360 Theme

- Fun and joy.

360 Environment

- The dance class.

360 Experience

- **Point of view.** The child joins the experience as if they are in the middle of everything. They'll feel like they are dancing with their friends.

- **Setup.** You place the 360 camera on a tripod in the middle of the dance floor. Next, you raise the tripod to about the eye level of the injured child.

  You're ready to go.

- **Recording.** As you press start on the phone app, the kids dance around the camera and start offering words of encouragement, telling their friend how much they miss them, and how they are looking forward to seeing them soon.

- **Uploading.** You drive over to the injured child's house and help upload the video to a parent's phone.

360 Delivery

- **Personal delivery.** You hand over a care package that includes a framed photo of the kids in the class, a card signed by everyone, instructions to view the experience, and a headset.

- **Viewing.** Before you leave, you help the parent figure out how to properly view the experience. Later that evening, the parent hands the child the care package. As they open it, they find a new headset and the other thoughtful goodies. At this point, the parent asks if the child misses their friends in dance class. Looking sad, the child says, "Yes." The parent then responds, "Would you like to visit them?" The child nods and the parent places the headset on the child's head so they can view the experience.

3. Prayers after a car accident. Let's look at our new tool's application in the event of a loved one recovering from a car accident. Their body is in the hospital, but their mind can be virtually transported somewhere else for support and encouragement.

This is an example of what is possible. Always get permission from the primary recipient's doctor before delivering your 360 personal experience.

Backstory. Your best friend was just in a car accident on the other side of the country, and there is just no way you can get there to support them. You throw your hands up in the air and feel completely helpless. As you talk to their spouse, you mention that you are praying for a fast recovery.

The spouse says, "Thank you so much!"

Like a light bulb going off in your head, you remember this chapter of this book and immediately jump into action. You gather your family and head over to the place of worship you both attended while growing up. With permission from your spiritual leader, you quickly gather friends and family and encircle the 360 camera near the altar. You press record on the phone app and begin to pray for a fast recovery and to offer support.

360 Recipients

- **Primary Recipient:** Your best friend.
- **Secondary Recipient:** None. This is only for the patient.

360 Theme

- 360 personal prayer experience for fast healing and emotional support (VR Prayer).

360 Participants

- Your family and the spiritual leader at the place of worship.

360 Environment

- The place of worship the two of you grew up in.

360 Experience

- **Point of view.** Your friend enters the experience as if they are standing in the middle of the prayer circle.

- **Setup.** Once your family arrives, you get permission to record the video. At this point, the spiritual leader is intrigued and accepts your request to say a prayer. Then everyone bunches up together near the altar to ensure your friend doesn't have to move to view the experience. Lastly, you place the 360 camera on a tripod and raise it to eye level.

- **Recording.** You press start on your phone's app. The spiritual leader gives a fantastic prayer for fast healing. In the middle of the leader's prayer, you decide your friend needs quiet time in this special place. Therefore, in the ten-minute video, the spiritual leader only prays for five minutes. The rest of the time is spent creating a quiet place for your friend to pray.

- **Uploading.** You're surprised at just how fast you can create and deliver an experience. Next, you decide to upload the video to your YouTube Channel as a private experience.

360 Delivery

- **Professional (medical) delivery.** You tell a member of your friend's family at the hospital where they can quickly purchase a headset. They are back in the hospital within twenty minutes. When it's ready to be viewed, the family member shows the nurse and doctor in charge the experience to get their permission to show it to the patient—your best friend.

- **Viewing.** After viewing the experience, the healthcare professionals prepare your friend to sit up in bed to see the experience. After this, the doctor gives the go ahead to place the headset on your friend's head. Immediately, your friend recognizes the environment and is grateful for the chance to pray from their hometown place of worship. Your friend breaks into a big grin as tears pour down their face.

2. Encouragement Examples

Next, you will view two examples of how to help your loved

ones and people in your community to receive encouragement from their loved ones around the world.

1. Prayer for change. Here's an example of how you can be supportive of a friend experiencing a change in their life. This experience is quite simple and can be duplicated for a multitude of experiences.

Backstory. A friend lost their job as a software developer more than a year ago. They weren't too worried about finding a new job because they thought everyone was looking for people with their skills. Over this time, your friend has been absent from the group and turns to you for support and encouragement.

360 Theme

- A message of encouragement so they can believe in themselves again during this transition.

360 Participants

- Friends and family.

360 Environment

- By the grill in your backyard.

360 Experience

- **Point of view.** Your friend in transition enters your experience feeling like they are in your backyard by the grill.

- **Setup.** As the experience unfolds, you ask everyone to stand around the 360 camera at eye level.

- **Recording.** When everyone is ready, you take your phone out and press start on the phone app. At this point, pre-selected participants in the group talk to your friend in a tough spot with words of encouragement.

- **Uploading.** Due to the privacy required, you decide only to record and upload the video to your phone.

360 Delivery

- **Personal delivery.** The next night, you head over to your friend's house and hand them a care package with a framed picture of the participants, a congratulations card from the group, instructions, and a new headset. What a great surprise since no one has seen their friend in quite a while!

- **Viewing.** As your friend puts on their headset, they will be virtually transported to your backyard. Every time your friend feels down, they will watch the immersive bridge to remind them they don't have to feel so isolated.

2. Life after divorce. Picking up the pieces after a divorce can be a daunting task. This example looks at how to work through divorce through a virtual reality experience.

Backstory. Your best friend's divorce is now final. You can begin to see them drifting away and becoming isolated. You both know it takes time to heal and trust again. You jump into action and create an immersive bridge to their favorite spot.

360 Recipients

- **Primary Recipient:** Your best friend.
- **Secondary Recipients:** Your Facebook friends. They get to join in the fun experience from around the country.

360 Theme

- This fun theme is a surprise video to remind your friend they are not alone and that they will get through this.

360 Participants

- This video includes only yourself.

360 Environment

- Your friend hasn't been to the ocean in a while. So you will create a surprise video that will bring them to their favorite spot by the pier.

360 Experience

- **Point of view.** Your friend will feel like they are at the beach with you.

- **Setup.** You place the 360 camera on a tripod with a perfect view of your friend's favorite spot with the sunset in the background. You raise the camera to eye level, and you are ready to go. Press start on the phone app and say what's in your heart.

- **Recording and uploading.** This recording is a live event on your Facebook page. As the video starts, all their friends on Facebook will begin to give encouraging comments.

360 Delivery

- **Personal delivery.** Before you headed off to the beach earlier, you handed your friend a headset with simple instructions on how to view the experience live in about an hour. You give them a text right before the live event starts on Facebook.

- **Viewing.** To view the experience, your friend cues up the experience on the phone and then slides the phone into the headset. Additionally, the guests on Facebook join in from your friend's point of view and post on your page as well.

- **Note:** You don't need to have a headset to view the 360 video. Your Facebook friends can simply move the video around with their fingers (or mouses) to view the 360 content.

3. Community Tragedy Example

Encouragement through a community tragedy. Up to this point, we have looked at examples with one primary recipient. In the next example, we'll look at how you can create an experience for a whole community. A goal of mine is one day to hear a first responder say, "This is awful. Send in the headsets and virtually get them out of there."

> A goal of mine is one day to hear a first responder say, "This is awful. Send in the headsets and virtually get them out of there."

Backstory. A few families on Elm Street have decided to hunker down after they hear the news of a fire in the nearby mountains. After an hour, they begin to smell something burning and quickly realize they are trapped. The families can do nothing until help arrives from the sky.

One of the potential victims decides to call their spiritual leader to create a 360 personal experience for everyone to share during this potential tragedy.

The spiritual leader creates an experience that virtually brings the families on Elm Street to a nearby community place of worship that is not in harm's way.

360 Recipients

- **Primary Recipients:** The families on Elm Street.
- **Secondary Recipients:** The families' loved ones from around the world watch this experience and feel great empathy for the families on Elm Street.

- **Strangers.** Strangers from around the world hear the story and find this virtual event on Facebook. Here, they can virtually join in a prayer of safety from the place of worship.

360 Theme

- A 360 (virtual reality) prayer experience for encouragement and safety.

360 Participants

- You (the local spiritual leader) and your prayer warriors.

360 Environment

- This experience takes place by the altar inside your local place of worship.

360 Experience

- **Point of view.** The families on Elm Street join the experience by entering from the point of view (POV) of being in the middle of the prayer circle at a place of worship that is not in harm's way.

- **Setup.** To get started, the prayer warriors quickly form a half-circle around the 360 camera. In this video, one half of the circle is composed of the 360 participants. The other half is the backdrop of the altar.

- **Recording.** You press start on the phone app and record a video to your Facebook page. In the video, the spiritual leader prays for the families in the danger zone, for the safety of the firefighters and other first responders, and for the consolation of the loved ones watching.

- **Uploading.** Once you have ended the recording, upload the ten-minute video to your Facebook page. Once that has been completed, you start telling everyone where to find the video and asking them to pray for the families, firefighters, and other first responders.

360 Delivery

- **Families on Elm Street have headsets.** A few of the families on Elm Street have their own headsets and share them with others in the area to view the experience.

- **Note:** I'm looking forward to the day when first responders administer reality tools as part of their aid. In this scenario, first responders will deliver the headsets to help alleviate stress in tough situations.

- **Viewing.** The families on Main Street will put on the headsets and feel like they are in a place of worship out of harm's way. As they continue to feel stress, they can "check out" of the real world and virtually head over to another place of worship as they see fit during tough times.

- **Family, friends, and neighbors (store bought).** Family members, friends, and neighbors of the families on Elm Street can don their own headsets to feel a part of this vitally time-sensitive prayer.

- **Viewing.** These secondary recipients can view the experience by simply placing on their headsets to join the prayer from a local place of worship.

- **Strangers from around the world (store bought).** As strangers here of this story, they head to their local electronics store to purchase a headset to help feel a part of the story from across the world.

- **Viewing.** Complete strangers will join in the prayer to support everyone's safety. These strangers may be across the world, but they will be connected in a way not available to them before reading this chapter.

4. Grieving Example

Favorite spot to grieve. The death of a loved one can be an earth-shattering experience that brings even the strongest to their knees. Here's an experience where you get out of the way and create an immersive bridge for the bereaved to spend quality time alone.

Many times, it's not the words we use but how we listen to what others need that is important.

Backstory. Your best friend's spouse just passed away. After the funeral, you can tell they are truly grieving. You quickly realize there is nothing you can say or do. However, after reading this book, you spring into action and bring them to their favorite peaceful spot to meditate.

360 Recipients

- **Primary Recipient:** Your friend in a time of significant emotional trauma.
- **Secondary Recipients:** None.

360 Theme

- A healing time of meditation at your friend's favorite place in the world.

360 Participants

- None.

360 Environment

- The dock of your friend's family cabin on a bright and quiet Sunday morning.

360 Experience

- **Point of view.** Your friend enters the immersive bridge and virtually travels to their favorite spot at the end of the dock. As your friend sits on a rotating chair, they spin around and feel like they are on the dock. This video gives them the space to grieve.

- **Setup.** Early one Sunday morning, you get the keys from your friend and head up to their family cabin. It's 8 a.m.—a perfect time to record a silent video off the end of the dock. You place the 360 camera on a tripod and raise it to your friend's eye level.

  Now that everything is set up, you hide so you are not in the experience.

- **Recording.** When you're ready, you press start on the phone app and record a quiet, ten-minute video with only nature's sounds in the background.

- **Uploading.** Upload the video to your phone.

360 Delivery

- **Personally delivered.** A few days later, you bring over a care package with a special present, cookies, headset, instructions on how to view it, and framed pictures of happier times.

- **Viewing.** When you come to deliver the experience, you get your friend's permission to upload the video to their phone from the 360 camera. After the upload, place your friend's phone in the headset and start the video. Your friend puts on the headset and can then spend time in peace at their favorite place. As they continue to grieve, they can watch this video hundreds of times to help them relax.

Chapter 6: Summary

You learned how to bring hope and encouragement to your family member, friend, or person experiencing difficult times.

Your personalized experience can offer encouragement during a difficult time.

You can help support a whole town during or after a community tragedy.

You learned how to help others grieve after a recent loss.

Chapter 6: Summary

Now it's your turn to create your own 360 personal experiences for others in difficult times. The following questions will help to point you in the right direction to get started.

360 Recipients

Primary Recipients: Who is your primary recipient(s)?

_____

_____

_____

_____

Who can you watch this immersive experience to support the primary recipient (secondary recipients)?

_____

_____

_____

Secondary Recipients: How would watching this video help the secondary recipient understand the primary recipient (walking in another's shoes)?

_____

_____

_____

_____

Time Recipients: How could this 360 video support the primary recipient five years from now?

_____

_____

_____

_____

360 Theme

What is the purpose/theme?

_____

_____

_____

_____

How will this video support your primary recipient(s)?

_____

_____

_____

360 Participants

Who will be in your video (360 participants)?

_____

_____

_____

What words will they use to be supportive?

_____

_____

_____

Who will you need to keep out of video?

_____

_____

_____

360 Environment

Where are you virtually bringing your primary recipient(s)?

_____

_____

_____

Describe the environment in detail?

_____

_____

_____

Will this environment be in the past, present, or their future?

_____

_____

_____

Why bring them there?

_____

_____

_____

360 Experience

How will you record your video?

_____

_____

_____

Will you upload your video to YouTube or Facebook?

_____

_____

_____

Will your video be recorded or live?

_____

_____

_____

What permissions will you need before recording?

_____

_____

_____

360 Delivery

How will you deliver your experience in person or mail it?

_____

_____

_____

What support will you need from the primary recipient's medical team?

_____

_____

_____

Chapter 7
360 Personal Experiences For Personal Growth

"All thoughts which have been emotionalized, (given feeling) and mixed with faith, begin immediately to translate themselves into their physical equivalent or counterpart."

NAPOLEON HILL

My goals have this funny way of repeating themselves every year. They usually include needing to finally get in shape, running that 5K, finding some new friends, and learning how to cook healthy foods. I think of the same goals every year. Why is that?

I have this hilarious annual ritual. I start the year by telling myself, "Forget about last year. This year I can do it." I run to the bookstore to get a new book on goal setting. Then I write my goals down in a fresh way and even put them up on my bathroom mirror. Most years, after a few weeks, I have given up on most of these goals. Does this sound like you? If so, can you tell me why we keep doing this to ourselves?

What's Missing

What was missing for me all these years was the belief that I could overcome my fears and walk in enough faith to win the prize. I could read my written goals thousands of times, but deep down, it was difficult for me to let go of my past hurts and failures.

I'm assuming this is the most challenging part of goal setting for you as well.

Personally, I don't feel I need better-written goals. I need to improve my deep belief that I can persevere and win.

This thought is how I learned to apply our new virtual reality tool to our dreams. Imagine if you could take the dream/vision picture off your loved one's wall and then turn it into a personalized and immersive virtual reality event for them from their own future. In this experience, they will feel like they have gone forward five years and achieved their goal. Chapter 7 has three main points:

1. What is a future experience?
2. Create an experience from the past to build references (going back in time).
3. Create a future experience to build faith.

What Is A 360 Dream (Vision) Board Experience?

> A 360 personal dream board experience is an immersive bridge to a person's past or future that helps their mind believe that they can reach their goals.

Going Backwards In Time (Build References)

With these new reality tools at your disposal, you can create immersive bridges to the past to build references to previous successes. Therefore, loved ones can use their own histories to gain the confidence to believe they can do it again. Here's one example to help illustrate.

Past examples. Creating a 360 personal dream board experience from your loved one's past seems very abstract at first. But imagine reliving a scene from your past that reminds you of a challenge you overcame or a goal you reached. Reliving this positive memory may help you build faith in yourself. This is the experience you're creating for the people in your life and your community.

Build faith after a job loss.

Backstory. Six months ago, your sibling suddenly lost their job. Their life was almost perfect; then everything changed. Your sibling is still struggling to find a new job, their savings have been depleted, and the bank is foreclosing on their home. After a tough phone call, you can tell they are falling into depression and losing hope, so you decide to ask what's next for them.

They say this might be a good time to go back to college, but in the same breath, they remind you how hard it was for them even to finish high school. You wish you could be with them in person, but it's impossible because they live on the other side of the country.

After only a moment's pause, you jump into action and decide to bring your struggling sibling back to the exact time and place where they decided to stay in high school and graduated with their friends.

To you, it sounds like they are reliving a similar crisis of confidence from the past.

360 Recipients

- **Primary Recipient:** Your sibling as they contemplate going back to finish college.
- **Secondary Recipients:** None.

360 Theme

- You're taking your sibling back to high school to the exact place where you discussed with them about dropping out of school. Out of that conversation, they decided to stay in school, and went on to graduate on time. The theme is to build faith by reliving a big win from the past.

360 Participant

- Only you.

360 Environment

- The parking lot of the high school you both attended. In this exact spot, they were thinking of dropping out of school. But this is also the place where they decided to stay in high school. Your sibling was struggling at that point, but they persevered and got the diploma. Your sibling instantly remembers this place.

360 Experience

- **Point of view.** Your sibling enters this experience standing next to you by your car with the high school in the background.

- **Setup.** Go to the high school parking lot and place your 360 camera on a tripod raised to about your sibling's eye level as you're standing up. It's that simple. You're ready to go.

- **Recording.** As you press start on the phone app, you begin to remind them of this spot and its significance to their past.

- **Uploading.** You decide to upload the video to YouTube and offer this as a private video link.

360 Delivery

- **Mailed.** After you upload the video, you head to the store to create a care package that includes a headset, instructions on how to view the immersive bridge, the private link, and an encouraging card reinforcing that they can go back and finish college successfully. Once the care package is complete, you mail the package to your sibling.

- **Viewing.** At your sibling's home, you help them set up the viewing. As your sibling puts on the headset, they know exactly where they are and why this spot is so important. As the experience unfolds, it helps them build faith that they can overcome again and finish that degree because they have overcome before.

Going Forward In Time (Goal Setting)

Next, let's dig into how you can take the dream board picture off the wall and make it come alive in a 360 personal dream board experience from the future.

Goal setting. I'm assuming you have read or are familiar with the classics of personal development and goal setting. I certainly can't improve on them, so I recommend you pick your favorite author and follow their direction. Moreover, I would strongly encourage you to find a personal development coach and let them help you create this dream of the future. Visit **www.vrformainstreet.com** to find a coach who fits your goals.

Types of goals. In creating these experiences, you can take people to their future to view an experience where they have achieved their dreams.

Here are just a few goals to get you started:

- Financial and business.
- Addiction recovery.
- Healing recovery.
- Weight loss/healthy living.
- New job or promotion.

Let's look at three examples to help you get started.

1. New business example. Starting a new business requires drive and conviction—and skills. This challenge can be daunting enough to prevent us from starting a new venture and seeing it through to the end. The struggle to believe in ourselves keeps most of us on the sidelines of our own lives, not living our real purposes. In this example, you'll learn how to create an experience for your loved ones to help them believe in themselves and to assure them they can leave a legacy of hope for their whole family.

Backstory. Your sibling has recently started a new business. You can tell they are beginning to struggle to maintain the original dream. You jump into action, first by grabbing some coffee with them. In that chat, you ask what their number one goal was when they started the business. They respond that they wanted to buy a new home where the kids would have a bigger backyard to play in. Your sibling becomes emotional when they say they would also like to spend more time playing in that backyard with the kids.

360 Recipients

- **Primary Recipients:** Your sibling.
- **Secondary Recipient:** Their spouse and children.

360 Theme

- Fun day in the new home.

360 Participants

- This experience includes you, your sibling's spouse, and their two children. That's it.

360 Environment

- You find someone with access to a house very similar to your sibling's dream house. This home has the perfect patio, deck, backyard, and firepit. You are ready to get started after receiving the proper permissions.

360 Experience

- **Point of view.** In your preparations, you decide to create a video where your sibling feels like they are standing on the deck of this new home watching their spouse and children play in their new backyard.

- **Setup.** To set up the experience, place the 360 camera on a tripod and then raise it to your sibling's eye level. Place the tripod at the end of the deck with a full view of the yard.

- **Recording.** Count out loud to five so everyone can get ready. Using the spouse's phone, press "start" on the app to begin the recording. In this ten-minute recording, you capture the three of them playing in the backyard. One-by-one, they come up to you on the deck. They congratulate your sibling on their success and talk about how happy they are that your sibling has so much time to play with them in their new backyard.

- **Uploading.** Next, you decide it would not be appropriate to upload the video to a social media site; therefore, you upload the video only to the spouse's phone.

360 Delivery

- **Personal delivery.** A few days later, on date night, your sibling's spouse and kids talk about your sibling's number one dream. During this special time alone, the spouse says the magic words, "Let's go there. Let's visit the future."

- **Viewing.** The spouse hands over a care package. In this wrapped package is a headset, a framed picture of everyone playing at the house, and a congratulations card dated for an appropriate time in the future. When your sibling puts on the headset, they travel through this immersive bridge to the dream home and watch the family play in their new backyard. Your sibling may watch this hundreds of times to build their faith that they can achieve their goal.

2. Top college example. In this next example, we look at how you can teach your child to believe they can attend the college of their dreams. This experience transports an ambitious high school student to their first day of college at Yale.

Backstory. Your child is a freshman in high school and dreams of becoming a top brain surgeon. In their spare time, they want to travel the world and help young children with brain trauma. In a recent conversation, they told you of their dream to attend Yale.

360 Recipient

- **Primary Recipient:** Your child (as a freshman in high school).
- **Secondary Recipients:** None.

360 Theme

- This experience will virtually transport your child to their first day of college at Yale; therefore, this theme is to help your child build faith in their dreams.

360 Participants

- This experience includes yourself, your spouse, and your eldest child.

360 Environment

- This future experience virtually brings your child to the main walkway leading up to Yale University.

- **Note:** You can certainly do your best to duplicate this experience at another college, but it is always best to create a real and authentic experience at the exact spot where you would like to virtually bring them.

360 Experience

- **Point of view.** As your child puts on the headset, they are virtually taken to Yale University.

- **Setup.** Out of your duffel bag, you grab your 360 camera and place it on the end of your selfie stick. To get started, you extend your arm out and put the camera at your child's eye level. You're now ready to begin.

- **Recording.** Count down from three and press start on the app on your phone. At this point, you, your spouse, and your older child start walking down the sidewalk, while you talk to the 360 camera as if it were your child. You congratulate them on arriving at their first day of college. Moreover, three other college freshmen join in your conversation to congratulate your child.

- **Uploading.** You decide only to upload the experience to your phone to show your child personally when you get home.

Afterward, you can download it to your computer to be edited and viewed later.

360 Delivery

- **Personal delivery.** When you return home, the three of you hand your younger child a congratulatory balloon and wrapped present. They open the present and seem intrigued by the headset. You connect your phone to the headset. Being younger than you, your child knows how to use it and takes it from there.

- **Viewing.** In this experience, your child is immediately taken virtually to Yale University with their parents and sibling walking toward the school, congratulating the younger child from the future they dream of. As the experience begins, you can see your child crying as they realize how much you all love and believe in their dream. Over the next two weeks, your child watches this video three times a day and begins to feel that they can do this.

3. Weight loss example. The following example shows us one way to use our new tools to build the confidence to lose weight.

Backstory. You are an aspiring servant-leader who has just received a promotion and wants to help create personal breakthroughs for all your employees. You not only care about the team members personally, but you know that building up others leads to a more successful organization.

360 Recipient

- *Primary Recipient:* This video is a story created for a team member who has struggled with weight since their spouse passed away three years ago. This person is a hardworking and loyal employee.

- *Secondary Recipients:* **Other team members may be inspired by this video and will start to look at creating a 360 personal dream board experience like this to help their friends and family members believe in their own goals.**

360 Theme

- This theme is a 360 personal dream board experience that may help your team member believe they can achieve their weight-loss goal. Additionally, the primary recipient may discover that they are well liked and appreciated at their workplace.

360 Participants

- The participants will be you and the team. In this experience, the 360 participants will talk to their coworker as if the coworker has already achieved their weight-loss goals in the near future. Their words may include congratulations, encouragement, and support.

360 Environment

- The virtual environment is a walking tour around the office, where coworkers congratulate the team member on losing weight.

360 Experience

- **Point of view.** This video is an experience for the team member walking down the hallway at work where everyone is congratulating them for hitting their goal weight.

- **Setup.** As supervisor, you prepare the six steps and present the idea to the team member for their approval.

Second, you call a quick meeting with your team to talk about this experience. After a quick conversation, everyone agrees to help. You can tell that coworkers are excited to begin the video. Without a moment's delay, you ask everyone to head back to their cubicles. From there, you start this breakthrough experience from your team member's "future."

Third, you place your 360 camera on your selfie stick and extend your arm as far as you can to ensure the camera is at eye level with your team member as you're walking. At this point, you're ready to get started.

- **Recording.** Press start on the phone app and begin to walk down the hall to talk with everyone in their cubicles. In these quick conversations, everyone offers their own unique congratulations and reasons why they like the team member so much. During the recording, a few work friends talk about how the team member's courage has also helped them.

- **Uploading.** You know how important and private this topic is, so after the video is recorded, you help upload the experience to the team member's phone only. Next, you delete the video from the camera. As a result, only one person, the primary recipient, has a copy of this recording.

360 Delivery

Personal delivery. The next day, you gather everyone in the conference room to deliver the experience as a group. Everyone applauds the team member's openness, and they all offer support. You then hand over a care package with a headset and instructions on how to view the experience.

Since this could be emotional, you recommend the team member watch the video later that night.

- **Viewing.** Later that night, in the privacy of their home, your team member views the immersive bridge to their future. They will be moved in a way that will inspire them to believe the office loves them. This could help in losing their weight. Even if they never lose the weight, it's possible this experience will make this team member a much happier, more productive, and long-term employee.

Chapter 7: Summary

A 360 personal dream board experience is an immersive bridge to a person's past or future that helps their mind believe they can reach their goals.

You learned how to bring another to their own past to relive a positive memory. This may help to build their faith that they can achieve their goal in their near or distant future.

You can now virtually bring another person to their own projected future. Here, the primary recipient will watch an experience where they have already achieved their goal.

Chapter 7: Worksheet

Creating a 360 personal dream board experience will look to build faith that someone can stay sober, believe they can walk again, fall in (or back in) love again, or hit a financial goal.

> A 360 personal dream board experience is an immersive bridge to a person's past or future that helps their mind believe that they can reach their goals.

Here's an exercise to get you into action today.

360 Recipients

Who would you like to support with a 360 personal dream board experience (primary recipient)?

_____

_____

_____

_____

Who else could watch this video to better understand your primary recipient(s)?

_____

_____

_____

_____

360 Theme

What is the intention of your future-orientated experience?

_____

_____

_____

_____

Who would this theme support the primary recipient(s)?

_____

_____

_____

360 Participants

Who would be the best people in your video?

_____

_____

_____

_____

Would this be a surprise party?

_____

_____

_____

What supportive and positive words would they use?

_____

_____

_____

360 Environment

Describe the place in the future.

_____

_____

_____

_____

360 Experience

How would you create and upload your video?

_____

_____

_____

_____

Will this be a live or recorded video?

_____

_____

_____

What permissions will need to record your video?

_____

_____

_____

360 Delivery

How would you present it to them (in person or mailed)?

_____

_____

_____

What would you include in your care package (if mailed)?

_____

_____

_____

Chapter 8
What Is A 360 Community Experience?

"The price of doing the same old thing is far higher than the price of change."

BILL CLINTON

Would you like your parent in assisted living to be able to virtually leave their room to attend a local concert? How can I deeply connect my business's target audience to my grand opening?

These are questions we will answer in Chapter 8.

A 360 personal experience is all about a personalized experience for one person, a group of people, or your very specific target audience.

By comparison, a 360 community experience has a much broader group of primary recipients. In other words, the primary recipients could be as large as everyone in your community.

In Chapter 8, you will learn:

- **What is a 360 community experience**
- **Who may create these experiences**
- **Six steps to creating your own community experience**

What Is A 360 Community Experience?

A 360 community experience is an immersive 360 video created for a large group of primary recipients. These primary recipients can be a whole community or a large target marketing audience.

Examples include a 360 video of a garden (with soothing sounds in the background), a silent place of worship, or a beach during a sunset.

These videos are meant for everyone to view.

Who May Create these 360 Community Experiences?

Support for local residents in difficult times. Organizations in your community can help create these community videos to support caregivers and virtual reality departments.

Volunteer organizations. Volunteer organizations in your local community can incorporate these immersive videos into their monthly activities.

Spiritual organizations. Local spiritual organizations can incorporate virtual reality into their outreach programs. These outreach programs could include volunteers in hospitals, hospices, senior/assisted living, prison outreach, and homeless outreach.

Virtual reality departments. This new virtual reality department may be tasked with creating 360 personal and community experiences. This department can focus on one genre (e.g., beaches) or tackle the creation of dozens of experiences. You will learn how to create your own virtual reality department in Chapter 9.

Larger target audience. Local businesses can easily create public relations and advertising messaging that virtually brings the community into their business for a plethora of reasons. I will cover this topic extensively in Part Four.

Grand opening tour. A business can virtually invite the community to experience their ribbon cutting and their grand opening.

Holiday message. Create a holiday message for the community with a walking tour of the downtown's holiday lights.

Six Steps To Creating Your Own Community Experience

Creating a 360 community experience follows the same six steps from Chapter 4. In reviewing these steps, we will focus on creating 360 videos for the people in your community going through difficult times. But the steps can equally be applied for your public relations and advertising campaigns.

1. 360 Recipients

- **Public primary recipients.** Public primary recipients are everyone in your community.

- **Private primary recipients.** Private primary recipients are people in your community who have access to private 360 community experiences. These 360 videos may be private only to a local hospital, for example. The only way to access this 360 video is by viewing it through the hospital virtual reality station.

  These recipients are treated as special because many community venues will want these videos to stay private. For example, a local place of worship may request that only local hospital patients can watch their virtual experience of the silent prayer time. In doing so, the place of worship could grant you access to the recording, but it cannot be used for public consumption or put on social media.

> Private primary recipients are people in your community who have access to private 360 community experiences.

- **Secondary and time recipients.** These recipients are not a concern in community experiences because they are not personal to a person or group.

2. 360 Themes

Next, let's explore the possible 360 themes. The possibilities are endless. I've broken them down into four categories: spiritual, meditation, motivational, and adventuresome.

Spiritual themes. With proper permission, you can record local places of worship. In these experiences, you can record four types of spiritual experiences to share in local hospitals, hospices, assisted living, recovery centers, homeless shelters, and even prisons.

- **Silent prayers.** Record 360 videos that virtually bring a patient or a senior/assisted living resident to silently pray from their local place of worship. As they place on their headset, they will feel like they are praying silently in the front row.

- **Holiday messages.** A local spiritual leader can record a powerful community message to different audiences during the holiday season. These 360 videos can be viewed throughout local hospitals, hospices, assisted living centers, and more. Possible messages include:

- Moving messages to patients in local hospitals.
- Loving messages to hospice patients.
- A message to seniors in senior/assisted living that they are not alone.

- **Evergreen hospital/hospice messages.** Local spiritual leaders can encourage local patients/residents with a positive message.

- **Spiritual services.** Local community places of worship can now virtually invite local patients and seniors in senior/assisted living centers to attend their services. As the patients' place on their headsets, they will feel like they are in the front row of the service.

Meditation themes. These themes could include meditation experiences that virtually bring a patient to a local place to meditate, relax, and reflect on their life. Here are a few examples:

- Sunsets/sunrises.
- Parks.
- Beaches.
- Mountaintops.
- Gardens.

You can enhance these experiences by adding the following to your 360 themes.

- **Sound therapy.** You can edit into the video soothing sounds of a local singer, ocean waves, a pianist, bell ringers, or music to enhance the video's immersiveness.

- **Aroma therapy.** You can look at adding aroma therapy to enhance the experience in your virtual reality department (Chapter 9). For example, a caregiver can ask their assisted living residents what their favorite aroma is, then the caregiver can activate that aroma as the resident watches the relaxing video of a local sunset.

- **Tactile therapy.** You could add tactile elements to your virtual reality station. For example, you can add sand to your station (room) to let the hospital patient put their feet in the sand as they relax on the virtual beach.

Motivational themes. People in your hometown can hear a word of motivation and encouragement from local leaders, celebrities, or others who experienced exactly what the primary recipient is going through.

- **High school football coach.** A high school football coach can give a powerful experience from the local high school locker room.

- **Doctor message.** In a private experience, a hospital patient could hear a moving message from a doctor at that hospital.

Adventure themes. A 360 community experience can take the viewer on a virtual exploration of their local community. Their body may be in the hospital room or senior/assisted living center, but their mind can feel like they are taking a nature hike. Here a few examples to get you started.

- **Hiking trails.** Create a hiking 360 community experience where a hospice patient can feel like they are walking their favorite hiking trails.

- **Museum tours.** With permission, you can create an experience where a homeless person in a shelter can take a tour of a local museum.

- **Community centers.** With permission, a community can record local concerts, plays, and other events at the community center.

- **Big events.** You can record larger community events throughout the year, such as the Fourth of July fireworks or the first lighting of the downtown Christmas tree.

3. 360 Participants

This step is vital. You will need to get permission from participants who will be in the video. These participants can be leaders in your community, singers, bell ringers, and more.

4. 360 Environment

With the advice from the community, you will be able to head out to create 360 videos that may support up to hundreds of people in your area.

5. 360 Experiences

Creating a community video is identical to the steps in Chapter 4 but with two additions:

- Make sure to purchase a 360 camera that can record live connections with Facebook and YouTube. This will help to virtually bring people in your community to a live stream of a community concert.
- I suggest that your public community experiences be free for others to use in your community.

6. 360 Delivery

The 360 delivery process is exactly the same as in Chapter 4.

Chapter 8: Summary

A 360 community experience is an immersive 360 video created for a large group of primary recipients. These primary recipients can be a whole community or a large target marketing audience.

Volunteer and spiritual organizations can incorporate these 360 community experiences into their monthly activities.

Virtual Reality Departments can look to create 360 community experiences as part of their monthly functions.

Local businesses can utilize these experiences in a public relations or advertising campaign.

This experience has two types of primary recipients:

1. Public primary recipients.
2. Private primary recipients.

There are four types of 360 themes. These themes can be created to be:

1. Meditative.
2. Spiritual.
3. Adventurous.
4. Motivational.

Chapter 8: Worksheet

Here are a few questions to help you create your own 360 community experiences.

Prayer

Where would be the best spiritual places to record in your community?

_____

_____

_____

_____

Why there?

_____

_____

_____

_____

Would this experience be silent or deliver a spiritual message?

_____

_____

_____

Meditation

Where could you virtually bring a hospital patient in your community to meditate?

_____

_____

_____

How would this location help them meditate and relax during a difficult time?

_____

_____

_____

_____

What music or nature sounds could support the experience?

_____

_____

_____

Encouragement

Who would be the best people in your community to record an encouraging or motivational speech?

_____

_____

_____

_____

Adventure

What are a few local adventure ideas in your area to record?

_____

_____

_____

Would this be a silent tour or require a tour guide?

_____

_____

_____

PART THREE

The Rise Of The Virtual Reality
Department

Chapter 9

The Rise Of The Virtual Reality Department

———

"The need for connection and community is primal, as
fundamental as the need for air, water, and food."

DAN ORNISH

Virtual reality allows us to connect with others in ways
unavailable to us before this new era. In Chapter 9, you will take
what you have learned and apply it to creating a new
department that will deliver these experiences to the people in
your community.

I've come to understand that this new technology will come into
our world partly by the same caregivers who serve the people in
your hometown today. These people include your local doctors,
nurses, volunteers, teachers, first responders, and spiritual
leaders. I am excited to start Part Three by offering your
community hope in the age of quantum computers, artificial
intelligence, automation, and nanotechnology.

In this chapter, you will learn how to embrace one of our new
reality tools to help support the people in your area in feeling
connected during times at a hospital, hospice, or
senior/assisted living facility. This can best be accomplished by
the creation of a local virtual reality department.

Here is what you will learn in Chapter 10:

- **What is a virtual reality department?**
- **Virtual reality department community standards.**
- **Functions of a virtual reality department.**
- **Virtual Reality Stations.**

What Is A Virtual Reality Department?

This new department will assume the leadership of your organization's virtual reality activities. This will be accomplished by creating a new department or establishing standards for your volunteer supporters.

By creating this department, you will have the opportunity to pioneer what is possible in your community by virtually bringing a patient or senior/assisted living resident to visit a loved one or to another location.

Here is the definition:

A virtual reality department is tasked with helping a hospital, hospice, senior/assisted living center, or other local organization that serves a community's residents. Support is provided through finding and creating pertinent, timely, and safe content to showcase at their facility. This content will include: 1. 360 personal experiences, 2. 360 community experiences, and 3. Safe virtual reality simulations. Next, this department will be tasked with safely delivering these experiences. This can be accomplished with the use of virtual reality stations.

Who should start a virtual reality department? Who is the frontline of making a virtual reality department a reality? The answer could be quite simple. It may be the same servant leaders who aid the residents where you live every day. These brave pioneers may be the first to showcase the possibility of helping to virtually connect their patients and senior/assisted living residents to:

- Their family members and friends.
- The outside world.
- The virtual (fantasy) world.

These immersive experiences will open up patients and their loved ones' minds to what's possible in our new era. None of us has a crystal ball. We don't have a full picture of what is ahead of us. The intention of the virtual reality department is to ensure that virtual reality is brought into our world to unleash our ability to connect in difficult times. Here's a small list of the new frontline of our new industrial era.

- Medical personnel (doctors, nurses, ambulance drivers).
- Assisted/senior living centers caregivers.
- Homeless shelter caregivers.
- Prison officers.
- First responders.
- Outreach centers.
- Spiritual leaders.
- Missionaries.
- Teachers.

Virtual Reality Department Community Standards

Next, let's look at what a virtual reality department may look like in your hometown. This section is only a starting point, and I'm looking forward to hearing from you about your opinions. As you begin, you may look to start a conversation with your community about virtual reality and its standards for care and other considerations. Visit **www.vrformainstreet.com** to join in this global conversation.

Standards of care. Countries around the world will have their own standards of how virtual reality may (or may not) be used. As you begin to investigate your department, you will need to understand and receive approval of your own medical associations for the use of virtual reality to support your patients, seniors, inmates, and the homeless. This book is designed to start that conversation with you. Here are only a few considerations to get the conversation started:

- **Research:** Your medical associations and insurance providers may require different levels of research and statistics to support your new department's initiatives.

- **Cleanliness:** Standards of passing or not passing headsets.

- **Viewing:** Standards for the delivery of your experience (placing on a headset) will vary from community to community.

- **Prior approval:** Your medical standards may require you to receive prior approval from the primary recipients' medical team before they view the 360 videos and virtual reality applications This may be vital as the experiences may cause dizziness, anxiety, or other potential hazards.

- **Post experience care:** Your medical standards may deem that your department meet a minimum level of care after an immersive experience. This may require a consultation to help bring the patient back to our real reality. This real reality that has no other realities attached to it.

- **Virtual Reality Stations:** You may be required to meet physical minimum requirements for your virtual reality mobile and static stations. This could include the size of the room, cleanliness standards, acoustics, electrical requirements, and other physical characteristics of the stations.

- **Payment:** Your facility will need to determine how to bill the patient for these services.

Ethical considerations. You may have to deal with many ethical considerations as you proceed with your new department. These considerations could include answering these questions:

- Is it ethical to take a patient on a virtual trip to their own place of worship?
- Is it ethical to virtually bring a patient forward or backward in their own lifetime?
- Is it ethical for a person's body to be in one place, but their mind (and heart) in another place?
- Is it acceptable to help alleviate a patient's feelings of isolation by sending them on a virtual trip?
- How many virtual trips will it take before a patient/resident prefers the virtual world over our real reality?
- Would it be ethical to have more friends in virtual reality than in the real reality?

> The real reality is our traditional reality where we interact with the physical world with no virtual, augmented, or holographic devices.

Cultural considerations. Culture considerations will vary city by city, and country by country. But as you begin to understand what is possible with virtual reality, your department may soon create experiences that will be viewed by people in multiple cultures (and countries). Keep in mind that people in many other countries may not be familiar with virtual reality and may not have evaluated their own cultural considerations.

Spiritual considerations. Your new department may need to start a conversation with your local spiritual organizations. In this conversation, you may mention your new department's goals and that you are looking to use this technology for good.

Language considerations. Your new department should look at creating experiences for patients who speak languages other than the primary language of your community. This most likely will require your department to look at creating one experience but in multiple languages.

Movements, sounds, and lights. Your department should consider previewing showcased virtual reality experiences for excessive movements, sounds, lights, or flashing of lights.

Hard of hearing and deaf considerations. Many in your community will have a hard time hearing or won't be able to hear your videos. I recommend you work with a professional in your area to edit your 360 videos. This editing should include text (scrolling text) as the 360 participants are communicating in the video.

Medical considerations. As you begin to plan your new department, you will need to seek the approval of your medical community before you begin any activities. Each community and country will have its own level of care requirements.

- **Medical conditions.** You (or the people recording the video) should not mention the patient's medical condition(s) in a recording. Make sure to follow your organization's privacy policies.

- **Patient information.** You should never disclose the patient's name, address, phone number, hospital, or other relevant, personal information. Always obey your state and country's privacy laws.

- **Outward experience only.** I suggest you virtually send an immersive bridge where a patient would leave their room and virtually travel somewhere else. I wouldn't suggest you bring the patient's family and friends virtually back to the patient's room.

- **Doctor's permission.** I recommend you receive the proper permission from the medical staff before delivering an immersive experience to your patient or senior/assisted living resident. This permission is vital because the medical team can evaluate the patient to see if they are physically and mentally fit to view a virtual reality experience. Unfortunately, these videos have the potential to cause dizziness, disorientation, nausea, strong emotional reactions, and more.

- **Counselors/mental health professionals.** Always get approval from the patient's mental health professional before showing the patient or senior/assisted living resident a personalized experience. Emotionally charged content could potentially bring up negative memories and other mental health issues that may inadvertently hurt the patient emotionally.

Delivery consideration.

- **Before viewing.** Deliver your 360 personal experiences with caution. These immersive experiences may be emotional and cause stress with the primary recipient. I suggest your department view the virtual reality experiences before your primary recipient watches them. Another suggestion is to have a list of preapproved experiences for the primary recipient to choose from.

- **During viewing.** It may be advisable for the medical team to monitor the primary recipient when they view the experience. This is important because the patient or senior/assisted living resident may begin to swing their arms, inadvertently walk around, turn around too quickly, accidentally trip, or even feel dizzy or nauseous.

- **Post viewing.** Your standards may require that you help the primary recipient after they have viewed an immersive experience. This will help the primary recipient come back to their real reality in a safe manner. These experiences have the potential to stir up physical and emotional reactions. Moreover, primary recipients may prefer the virtual experiences and become agitated or depressed when coming back to their real reality.

Administrative considerations.

- **Medical waivers (volunteers and staff).** Work with your business's legal team before starting your new department. Your legal team will advise you on your business's waivers from the primary recipient, their loved ones, and supportive volunteers.

Content ownership.

- **360 personal experiences.** Your new department may need to clearly identify who owns the newly created 360 personal experience. I would suggest that in most cases, the family member or friend who created the experience would own their own content, and they can disseminate the video in the fashion they see fit.

- **360 community experiences.** Your department may need to decide who owns the 360 community experiences your department creates. After the recording, your department can look to hire a local 360 video editor to add in the appropriate disclaimers, copyright protection, logos, and website links. These experiences can be viewed privately in your virtual reality stations or publicly on your social media.

- **Content sharing.** I suggest your department work with your legal team on disseminating 360 personal and community experiences. Sharing these precious moments should be done with care and compassion, especially since many of these experiences may go viral due to their emotional content.

How the primary recipient will view the experience. I suggest the medical team or caregiver give their assessment of how the virtual reality experience will be viewed by the primary recipient.

- **Standing up.** The patient or senior/assisted living resident can safely view the video standing up and rotating in a 360 degree circle.

- **Rotating stool.** Another option is to have the medical team help the patient sit down on a rotating stool. Here the primary recipient can spin around to view the 360-degree experience.

- **Bedside/sitting.** In many instances, the primary recipient will need to be seated on a chair or in bed. With that in mind, the person recording the experience will need to gather the 360 participants in close proximity. In doing so, the patient can view everyone talking without having to move their body (or head).

- **Bedside/lying down.** As with sitting down, a medical professional can place the headset on their patient so they can view while lying down on their bed. The 360 personal and community experiences will need to be recorded and edited in a manner that would support the patient's viewing.

Functions Of A Virtual Reality Department

As we looked at earlier, the role of a virtual reality department is to create and showcase experiences for the people in their care. There are three functions for this department.

1. Create 360 personal experiences. Supporting the personal connections between your primary recipient with their loved ones and the outside world will be a primary function of your new department. Here are only a few suggestions of what's possible.

- An assisted living center patient would like to spend Sunday dinner with grandkids in another city.
- A hospital patient wants to spend time with a sibling in Minnesota on New Year's Eve.
- A hospice patient would like to spend Valentine's Day with their child who lives in Brazil.
- A soldier is on tour in Japan. After permission from the commander, the soldier joins family back home for Thanksgiving dinner in Oklahoma.
- In your assisted living center, you realize you would like to be with your grandkids while they open their presents on Christmas morning. This experience brings you virtually to the Christmas tree.

2. Create 360 community experiences. Your department's second role will be to create 360 community experiences. It is recommended that this new department edit these videos for branding, upcoming events, logos, your copyrights, and credits. It is imperative that you receive the proper permissions before you record and upload these 360 videos. These permissions could be from the venue, bystanders, musicians, actors, and copyright holders. 360 community experiences can be summed up in the following four categories:

- **1. Meditation**
  - Beaches to relax.
  - Local garden to meditate.

- **2. Spiritual**
  - Places of worship to pray.
  - Hear a holiday message from a spiritual leader.

- **3. Outdoor & Adventures**
  - Hiking trails to get away
  - Museum tours to learn something

- **4. Motivational**
  - Motivational message from a high school football coach.
  - Hear a motivational speech from a famous person.

3. Virtual reality applications (simulations and games). An additional function of your department may be to search for the top and most appropriate virtual reality applications to showcase at your facility. These applications are not 360 videos. They are fully interactive simulations and games. These experiences put the viewer in control of where they move and how they interact with the simulation. In a 360 video, the primary recipient can only pause, play, rewind, or fast forward.

I suggest you review these applications prior to showcasing them at your virtual reality station. I am not here to judge. My only advice is that your applications reflect your community's ethical, cultural, and spiritual considerations. Here are a few things to consider in your assessment of content that doesn't meet your community's standards:

- Adult content.
- Violent acts.
- Respecting of others.

Virtual Reality Stations

A virtual reality station is where your patient or senior/assisted living resident will safely view the immersive experiences.

Static virtual reality station. A static virtual reality station is a secure station where a caregiver can safely deliver an experience for a patient or resident to view. This station can be placed in a private or public setting. Supervision will depend on the patient and the amount of care required. Here is what could be included in the static station:

- Gaming desktop computer.
- High-end headsets (a new headset for each primary recipient would be advised).
- Headset liners and cleaners.
- List of 360 experiences to view.
- Sign explaining how to use the station.
- Disclaimers to be signed before viewing.

- **Private static station.** A private static station may be in a secluded corner or its own room where the primary recipient can properly view an experience safely.

A private static station is a safe and private place to view 360 personal experiences, 360 community experiences, or VR simulations.

- **Public static station.**

  - **Primary recipient.** A public static station may be in a public area. Here, patients and seniors in senior/assisted living can access the virtual reality content in the cafeteria or other public places in your facility.

  - **Visitors.** Your facility can create a public station that can be accessed by your primary recipient's visitor. Many times,

- visiting loved ones in a hospital, hospice, or assisted living facility can be stressful. These visitors can have access to your experiences as well.

As they don their headset, they can take a virtual trip to relax, pray, or get away for a moment. Setting up an area for a visitor to watch television is a great choice. But it's conceivable that this public static station could also improve a visitor's experience. These headsets could be rented or purchased from your gift shop.

A public static station is a safe and public place to view 360 personal experiences, 360 community experiences, or VR simulations.

- **Mobile virtual reality station.** This station is mobile and can be delivered to an individual room or requested place in your facility. Here is a list of suggestions for your required equipment.

  - Table to place your computer, headsets, and other related equipment.
  - Table liner.
  - High-end gaming laptop computer.
  - High-end headsets (a new headset for each primary recipient would be advised).
  - Headset liners and cleaners.
  - List of experiences to view.
  - Disclaimers to be signed before viewing.

A mobile virtual reality station is mobile and can be delivered to an individual room or to be showcased in a public relations event.

- **Themed room.** The last way to deliver an immersive experience is to create a safe room that has a theme. For example, a local surfing club can create a surfing-themed room for a local children's hospital. This is a safe room where the child can be placed in the room with sand; the room can be made to look like the ocean (painted), smell like the ocean, and even sound like the ocean. As the young patient settles into the sand, the patient's parents or the doctor can place on the headset and the young patient will instantly feel like they are surfing the local waves. Visit **www.vrformainstreet.com** for more information on a themed room.

Chapter 9: Summary

A virtual reality department is tasked with helping a hospital, hospice, senior/assisted living center, or other local organization that serves a community's residents. Support is provided through finding and creating pertinent, timely, and safe content to showcase at their facility. This content will include:

1. 360 personal experiences.
2. 360 community experiences.
3. Safe virtual reality simulations.

Next, this department will be tasked with safely delivering these experiences. This can be accomplished with the use of virtual reality stations.

Local caregivers may be the frontline, bringing virtual reality into our real world.

Each community will have its own standards of care.

Every country will have its own ethical, cultural, and spiritual considerations.

Your department should consider editing your experiences to respect the people in your community who speak another language, have a hard time hearing, or can't hear.

It would be wise to preview every showcased virtual reality experience for excessive movements, sounds, lights, or flashing of lights.

Work with your facility to respect your patient's privacy and to receive permission from the primary recipient's medical team.

Monitor the primary recipient beforehand, during the viewing, and after the viewing to make the experience safe both physically and emotionally.

You will need the appropriate waivers as your department ramps up. Transparency will be required in who owns the video and its future dissemination.

The medical team will advise you on how the primary recipient will be able to view the experience. An experience can be viewed standing up, rotating in a chair, sitting down on a chair (not moving), or lying in bed.

There are three types of virtual reality stations:

1. A static station (private and public).
2. A mobile station.
3. A themed room.

Chapter 9: Worksheet

Here are a few questions to consider when starting your virtual reality department.

VR Department Considerations

What ethical questions will you need to address?

_____

_____

_____

_____

What community standards will be relevant to a new department?

_____

_____

_____

What spiritual questions do you have?

_____

_____

_____

_____

VR Department

What are you most excited about with this new department?

_____

_____

_____

How could this department improve patient satisfaction scores?

_____

_____

_____

How could you measure the department's effectiveness?

_____

_____

_____

Would you staff this department or look to incorporate volunteer groups?

_____

_____

_____

How much and what kind of training will you need?

_____

_____

_____

Think Big. Start Small.

Where would be the best department to start?

_____

_____

_____

Why that department?

_____

_____

_____

Who would lead the project?

_____

_____

_____

What do you need to get started?

_____

_____

_____

Chapter 10
Open Your Eyes To A New World

"We need more kindness, more compassion, more joy, more laughter. I definitely want to contribute to that."

ELLEN DeGENERES

Imagine if your family member could close their eyes and open them to be in another place during a difficult time in a hospital stay. Where would they like to visit? Chapter 10 answers this simple question. After reading this chapter, your hospital can start the conversation about making this virtual trip a reality. It is my assertion that many people will first experience virtual reality in a hospital setting. During this time, patients and their loved ones will learn to connect in ways that were unavailable to them before their stay.

As a leader at your hospital, it will be up to you to decide whether your hospital will be an early adapter or wait for others to work through virtual reality's early development. If you decide to come on board later, this book and the book's website, **www.vrformainstreet.com**, are here to support you when you're ready to jump in. If you're looking forward to leading the way, I wrote this next chapter to help start a conversation with you about what's possible with your leadership.

This chapter is written specifically for two types of hospital leaders:

1. Early Adopters: Your leadership is already paving a way for virtual reality at your hospital. I wrote this chapter to augment what you are currently doing or to offer a new insight to what is possible. This book is written at a high level and is not intended to overwhelm the executive with statistics and research.

2. Newcomers: Your hospital is beginning to investigate virtual reality and its possibilities for your facility. This chapter will help you start a conversation with your administration and community.

Now, let's dive in and explore how your hospital patients can take a virtual trip. Here is what you will learn in this chapter.

- **Goals of your virtual reality department.**
- **Important considerations.**
- **360 personal experiences.**
- **360 community experiences.**
- **Top virtual reality applications.**
- **Virtual reality department stations.**

Goals Of A Virtual Reality Department

Every new department starts with the best of intentions. At some level, the department will need to be measurable and bear fruit. Here are a few primary and secondary goals to consider when you look to add or create virtual reality functions at your facility.

Primary goals. Virtual reality is new to our world, so not enough empirical proof exists yet of a virtual reality department's return-on-investment (ROI). But together, we can help to explore its possibilities and investigate ways to gather the appropriate studies you may need. To get started, here's a look at two possible primary goals:

1. **Increase patient satisfaction scores.** Throughout this chapter, you will explore the possibilities of how virtual reality can potentially increase your patient satisfaction scores

2. **Increase key performance indicators (KPIs).** Every hospital is stretched, so every dollar must be evaluated for performance. As you build out your new department, make sure to include measurable results to ensure its effectiveness.

Secondary goals. Building out your new department will allow you to develop secondary goals for your executive team and your hospital. These goals may involve your leadership style, create public relations opportunities, improve staff morale, and increase volunteer support. Here's a look at a few potential secondary goals.

- **Lead from the front.** As we head into our new era, our world needs leaders to step up and showcase how we can be fearless in using technology for the good of us all. This effort will only take a few of us. Together, we can move this idea forward into the world.

> As we head into our new era, our world needs leaders to step up and showcase how we can be fearless in using technology for the good of us all.

As you begin your new department, you and your team are illustrating to the world that humans will prevail in this new era. We will use all its available tools to learn to thrive. This is the main mission of the Virtual Reality for Main Street Movement. Therefore, you are not creating just a cute nature video. You are helping to take a stand for your community.

- **Lead with the heart.** This department will allow you the space to lead with your heart. As a result, you can look to share and inspire your staff, patients, and community in general. Virtual reality may be the best empathy machine ever invented. You can now utilize its potential uses to serve your patients.

- **Become a regional and global thought leader.** Virtual reality is new to our world. Many of its best inventions and applications are still in front of us. With your leadership, you and your team can look at becoming global thought leaders. This may be possible as you embrace the ideas in this book or answer other questions related to this topic.

- **Public relations.** As you begin, you will have the ability to lead from the front and with your heart. This alone should help you create local, regional, and global headlines of how you are embracing our new reality tool to care for your patients. These TV, radio, podcast, and print interviews can include the following potential storylines:

  - How creating an experience supported a patient.
  - How/why your department started.
  - Doctor interview of the positive possibilities of this type of care.
  - Doctor interview focused on possible harmful effects of this type of care.

- **Legacy makers.** As you learned in the last chapter, your new department could conceivably leave a legacy for a family for decades to come. This legacy will showcase how a family can use the tools of our new era to unleash their ability to stay connected in times of joy and difficulty.

Then, they can use what they learned at your hospital to stay connected for decades to come.

- **Employee moral.** Creating these experiences may allow your team to lead with their heart. Consequently, your employee morale may increase because you have given them new tools to care for their patients. This new department could help spark the hearts of your entire staff.

- **Volunteer organizations.** As you roll out this department, you could see a rise in volunteers and volunteer organizations to support you.

  For example, a spiritual organization may learn the possibilities of 360 personal and community experiences. As a result, they may want to jump in and start assisting with your department.

Important Considerations

Before you begin your new department, you may want to consider a few things.

Budget and planning. Virtual reality equipment advances are made almost every month. It's unrealistic to prepare a budget for your department at this point because pricing and equipment change rapidly. Visit vrformainstreet.com for the latest recommendations and prices.

Grants. This book's online community will be searching all available sources for grant monies to conduct research on virtual reality's effectiveness for hospital care.

Privacy. Be advised of your community and organization's privacy standards. These will vary country by country.

Now, let's switch over and explore your new department's functions.

360 Personal Experiences

Your virtual reality department will be tasked with supporting your patients in taking a virtual trip to a place in their past, present, or future. These 360 personal experiences could improve your patient satisfaction surveys by potentially alleviating your patients' anxiety levels.

Family/friends support. Creating personal experiences will require the support of the primary recipient's family, friends, or volunteers. They will be required to create the 360 personal experience(s). Remember that this experience is about virtually bringing your patient somewhere else.

So you will need to work with your patient's family and friends to create the virtual destination for your patient to travel to.

Note: Fundraising and local organizations may look to raise money for the equipment necessary to create this experience.

Role of facilitator. Your new department may look to become the facilitator in helping your patient's family and friends create these experiences. You can look to accomplish this in an active or passive manner.

- **Active role.** Your new department can staff or find volunteers who would like to support your patient's family in the creation of these experiences.

- **Passive role.** A passive role will allow your department to steer people who wish to create these videos to a webpage or to purchase this book.

  - **Hospital website.** Your department can provide your own online support tools.

- **This book's website.** You can direct these family members and friends to **www.vrformainstreet.com** for resources to support their 360 videos.

Types of experiences.

- **Past experiences.** Virtually bring your patients back to an important place from their past. This could offer the patient the opportunity to:

  - Remember previous victories.
  - Reflect on old positive memories.

- **Present experiences.** Your department can virtually bring your patient to another place in the present. This could include bringing them to:

  - Their mother's kitchen table for dinner.
  - A place to pray, such as their own place of worship.

- **Future experiences.** Your team can virtually bring patients to their projected future to build their faith that they can recover from their accident, addiction, ailment, or surgery. Examples could include:

  - A future birthday celebration.
  - A loving message from their family celebrating their healing from their car accident.

Department examples.

- **Pediatrics example.**

  - A young patient could have dinner with their grandparents who live across the country.

- A young patient can feel like they are playing soccer with their own friends before an upcoming treatment.

- **Orthopedics example.**

  - A patient can feel like they are walking on the beach with their own family in the future.
  - The patient can run a virtual 5k with their friends.

- **Cancer care example.**

  - A patient can meditate or pray at the top of their favorite hiking spot as they watch the sunset.
  - A cancer patient can spend time at their parent's dock overlooking the water as they look to begin chemo treatment.

- **Recovery example.**

  - A person in recovery can view a future five-year sobriety party with their family and friends.
  - A recovering patient can go back to the past and relive a positive memory to help restore faith in themselves.

360 Community Experiences

Your virtual reality department can venture out into the community and record a plethora of local experiences. These experiences can be helping the patient to meditate, pray, be adventuresome, or be motivated. Going to Paris can be a great choice for a long-distance virtual trip. But many times, a patient may only want to travel to somewhere familiar in their local area.

- **Department examples.**

- **Emergency room examples.**

  - A patient can pray from a local place of worship.
  - A newly arriving patient can relax at a local beach.

- **Birthing examples.**

  - An expecting mother can watch a relaxing 360 video of a local streaming river prior to her appointment.
  - An anxious, expecting mother can hear a pianist in the background as she meditates on the top of a local mountaintop.

Top Virtual Reality Applications

Applications can take the patient on a virtual simulation of a beach, watch a 3D movie on Mars with their sibling, play an engaging video game, or skydive over Hawaii. New virtual reality content becomes available every month. Again, these are not 360 videos. They are immersive simulations where the patients are in control of how they interact with the environment. Visit **www.vrformainstreet.com** for a list of recommend applications.

Virtual Reality Department Stations

Virtual reality stations are a great choice for safely delivering immersive experiences to your patients. To learn what a station may look like, I would suggest visiting a local virtual reality gaming room. Here, you and your team will learn how to play virtual reality games and learn what is possible in a virtual reality station. Visit **www.vrformainstreet.com** for more answers on creating your own virtual reality stations.

- **Static stations.**

- **Public static station for the patient.** A public static station is a public area where patients can view 360 personal experiences, 360 community experiences, and virtual reality applications. For example, this station could be in the cafeteria, overlooking the lake, or in a reception area. All the patient will need is their own virtual reality headset to connect with the station's computer. This headset can be brought in by a loved one, or your hospital can provide this as part of their care.

- **Public static station for the patient's support.** Being in a hospital setting can also be stressful for the patient's family members and friends. In a public station, these family members and friends can take a virtual trip to the beach to meditate or to pray from a local place of worship. This virtual trip could help them in their support of the patient.

  To get started, they can purchase or rent a cleaned virtual reality headset to plug into the station computer.

- **Private static station.** This station will need to be in a safe and quiet place in the hospital. An example would be to have a private station at the end of each floor. This private station could be in a quiet place in the hallway or in a room by itself. In this setting, a patient can safely and quietly enjoy an immersive experience with their own headset plugged into the computer.

- **Mobile station room to room.** A mobile station can be easily be rolled (or moved) to a patient's room or another location in the hospital. For example, a local volunteer spends her Saturday bringing all the doctor-approved patients on the third floor on a thirty-minute trip to a local beach to relax.

- **Mobile station public relations.** A mobile station can be used in your public relations. You can easily bring this station to an upcoming speech in your community. After the event, you can ask the audience to line up and view the trip to this local beach for themselves.

- **Themed rooms.** The last type of station to create is a series of themed virtual reality rooms. These rooms will allow patients a safe place to feel like they have taken a virtual trip. Here are two idea starters for your new department:

  - **Paris.** The patient will enter the room to feel like they are in downtown Paris. The room is painted with 3D imagery, has a French table, smells like Paris, and has the exact sounds of a busy street. Next, the hospital patient stands in the room and places on the virtual reality headset. Immediately, they are walking through the streets of Paris.

  - **Local beach.** The patient on a wheelchair is rolled into a themed room of a Southern California beach. The air smells like the beach, the room looks like the beach, and it even sounds like the beach. The nurse closes the door and the patient places on the headset to feel like they are lying on the beach a whole world away.

Chapter 10: Summary

This department will allow you and your staff to become global thought leaders.

Your department will have the ability to create newsworthy stories for local media.

Your staff can create a legacy by helping a family embrace technology to unleash their ability to connect.

This department can potentially help improve employee morale.

You may see a rise in volunteer support.

There are some considerations before you begin, including budgeting, planning, and projected grant funds.

You may find this department as a bother to your daily functions.

A function of your department is to create and find pertinent, timely, and safe content to be viewed.

Virtual reality stations are the best way to deliver your approved 360 personal experiences, 360 community experiences, and virtual reality simulations.

Chapter 10: Worksheet

Here are a few questions to start developing your 360 virtual reality hospital department.

Starter Questions

What ethical and spiritual questions will you need to address?

_____

_____

_____

What are your community standards?

_____

_____

_____

What legal questions will you need to explore?

_____

_____

_____

What do you need to get started? i.e., research

_____

_____

_____

Development

What are you most excited about in the possibility of creating your own virtual reality hospital department?

_____

_____

_____

Which department would be an excellent place to start?

_____

_____

Why this department?

_____

_____

_____

What would you need to measure the department's effectiveness?

_____

_____

_____

What are your research and grant opportunities?

_____

_____

What training and support would you require?

_____

_____

_____

Volunteer Support

Which local organizations can assist you?

_____

_____

_____

_____

How could you raise the money needed to get started?

_____

_____

_____

_____

More Competitive

How could you best utilize a VR mobile station to promote your new department in your community?

_____

_____

_____

How could you incorporate empathic messaging into your public relations?

_____

_____

_____

Chapter 11
Grant Virtual Reality Last Wishes

———

"Together we can change the world, just one
random act of kindness at a time."

RON HALL

"Where would you like to go?" Your staff will be able to ask their patients this question once you develop your virtual reality hospice department. As you have learned, your patients can mentally and emotionally leave their hospice room by viewing a 360 personal or community experience.

As you have learned so far, your hospice can now unleash your patients' ability to feel connected with loved ones and with their favorite memories. Their bodies may be in hospice care, but their minds (and hearts) can feel like they are a world away. I like to think of this as granting a last wish.

As I see it, sending a card is an excellent choice, and it's fantastic to say a prayer, but the patient wants, above all else, to be with their loved ones during hospice care. I can't imagine a more beautiful gift from technology than to help you solve this problem. Solving this problem is the intention of this chapter.

In this chapter, you will learn how your hospice organization can create a virtual reality department that will grant last wishes to your hospice patients. Here's a list of the topics we will cover in this chapter.

- **Goals of a virtual reality department.**
- **Considerations.**
- **360 personal experiences (three stories).**
- **360 community experiences.**
- **Virtual reality applications.**
- **Virtual reality stations.**

Goals Of A Virtual Realty Department

To help get you started, here are a few potential objectives for your new department. For consistency, let's stick with the primary and secondary goals of the virtual reality hospital department.

Primary goal. To increase patient satisfaction, the success of which will be determined through patient surveys and key performance indicators (KPIs).

Secondary goals. Secondary goals will help to clarify what is possible for your department. Before we move on, here is the list from the previous chapter.

- Lead from the front.
- Lead with the heart by giving your team a new reality tool to use.
- Become a regional and global thought leader
- Create family legacies.
- Improve employee moral.
- Increase support from volunteer organizations.

In addition, let's add two more secondary goals specifically for your hospice.

- **Public relations.** You and your staff can bring your virtual reality mobile station out into the community to showcase how you are helping your patients through virtual reality. After the event, you can start a line and have local people in your community view the experiences you provide to your patients.

- **Fundraising.** As you're leading from the front and your heart, you can create viral social media videos. These videos will showcase the impact you are having on both your patients and your patient's loved ones. As always, I strongly suggest you receive the proper permissions before posting any videos on social media.

Considerations

Your department may need to answer potential questions as your programs rolls out. Here's a list of considerations from the last chapter:

- Budget and planning.
- Grants.
- Privacy.

Here are a few additional considerations for your new hospice department.

Timeliness. In creating a 360 personal experience, remember that timeliness is vitally important. These experiences can be created and delivered to your patients within hours if the patient's family and friends know how to create an experience. This speed will take a few weeks of practice to help facilitate.

No family members or friends. Decide if your department has the bandwidth to create 360 personal experiences for the people in your facility who don't have any support in creating a personal experience.

Position of viewing. 360 personal and community experiences will need to be made for your patients who will be standing, sitting, or lying down. The person creating the immersive bridge will need to act accordingly in the creation of the 360 videos. For example, if a patient watches the experience sitting down without turning, the video will need to be created with the 360 participants close together.

Delivery comfort. Medical staff will need to determine if the patient can physically wear the headset without interfering with medical equipment.

Emotional support. Living in one reality and coming out of another reality may cause unintended emotional stress. I suggest the primary recipient receive emotional support after the viewing.

Volume. Your team will need to practice with the loudness of your experiences for proper viewing.

360 Personal Experiences (three stories)

Your virtual reality department can now send your patients on a virtual trip to visit their past, visit loved ones in the present, or visit important places in the present. Let's take a deep dive into three examples of how you can quickly facilitate these experiences for your patients. Responsibility for the creation of these 360 videos will fall onto the family members and friends who cannot physically be with their loved ones.

The three stories backstory. Your loved one has lost their battle with cancer. They are on their way to a local hospice center. When they arrive, you gently take their hand and ask if there is anywhere they would like to go. The following three examples take them around the country to spend time at their favorite places.

One more trip around the lake. Where would you go if your life was coming to an end? What if you could go to those special places from a whole world away? This video is a 360 personal hospice experience.

Backstory. Your loved one arrives to start their hospice care. You ask where your loved one would like to go; they pause for a second and say they would like to take one more trip around the lake at the family cabin. You look at each other and shrug, knowing this is impossible. At this moment, your adult child enters the room and knows what to do. Without hesitation, they take action to make this virtual trip a reality.

360 Recipient

- **Primary Recipient:** Your parent in hospice care.
- **Secondary Recipients:** Other family and friends who cannot be there at this time.

360 Theme

- One more trip around the lake.

360 Participants

- A friend who lives in a cabin by the lake year-round.

360 Environment

- On a boat cruising the lake in front of the cabin.

360 Experience

- **Point of view.** Your loved one enters this experience as a passenger on the boat.

- **Setup.** You call your friend at the lake, who agrees to help make this experience. Picking up a 360 camera from the local store, your friend places it securely on a selfie stick. Next, your friend and a helper head down to the boat and drive out onto the lake. The helper holds the selfie stick firmly at (about) your loved one's eye level. They're ready to get started.

- **Recording.** Your friend drives slowly as his helper presses start on the phone app. In the last step, they record the trip around the lake, making a ten-minute video.

- **Uploading.** After recording, the two friends from the lake call the adult child from the boat and get help uploading the video to one of their Facebook pages.

360 Delivery

- **Primary Recipient: professional delivery.** Your friend on the lake has uploaded the video, and you're ready to deliver the experience to your loved one. Your adult child grabs their headset from the car and passes it to the nurse to gently place on your loved one's head.

- **Viewing.** As the video starts, your loved one instantaneously knows where they are and begins to cry as they say goodbye to one of their favorite places. Others can join in by watching this video created for your loved one.

- **Secondary recipients – family and friends: store bought.** Family and friends can view the experience in virtual reality by purchasing value headsets (about $20) from a local electronics store.

- **Viewing.** Family and friends will simply place their headsets on to feel a part of this important memory.

A special place to visit. A 360 personal or community experience can take us anywhere.

Backstory. Everyone is completely overwhelmed at the speed of the lake video's completion and its effect on your loved one. At this point, the family rushes to think of other places for your loved one to visit. You take your loved one's hand and gently ask if there is somewhere else they would like to go virtually? They pause for a second, cry a bit, and say they would like to visit the spot where they got engaged all those years ago. It seems like it's impossible, but your adult child knows how to do this. Since your loved one's spouse passed a few years ago, your loved one hasn't been back to that spot.

360 Recipient

- **Primary Recipient:** Your loved one.
- **Secondary Recipients:** Family and friends.

  - **Family and friends.** Those who cannot be there but can watch virtually on social media.

  - **Volunteers.** Hospice volunteers hear about this immersive bridge and wonder how they can offer this to other patients. Be ready to help them learn how they can create these experiences for others.

  - **Medical Staff.** The medical team can monitor the experience and look at potentially offering this as genuine care for other patients.

360 Theme

Personal reflection and prayer at the exact spot your loved one and their spouse got engaged sixty years ago.

360 Participants

- Local family members and your loved one's spiritual leader.

360 Environment

- The bench by the lake where the loved one and spouse got engaged.

360 Experience

- **Point of view.** Your loved one enters the experience as if they are sitting down at the exact spot where they got engaged.

- **Setup.** Everyone gathers around the bench. You place the 360 camera on a tripod and set it on the left side of the seat.

  Then you raise it to your loved one's eye level with a person sitting down next to it. That's it.

- **Recording.** You press start on the phone app and begin to record the event. In the recording, everyone gets to say what is in their hearts. But to begin, the first half of the video is of silence to let your loved one reflect on where they are and how this particular spot is one of their favorite memories.

- **Uploading.** After the recording is complete, you immediately upload the video to your Facebook page for everyone to view.

360 Delivery

- **Primary Recipient: professional delivery.** With your loved one's doctor's permission, you hand the prepared headset to the nurse who gently places it on your loved one's head.

- **Viewing.** Your loved one quickly knows where they are, and you begin to see the tears flow out of the headset. Your loved one takes the headset off and says, "I felt like I was there on the bench just like all those years ago." After a moment of disbelief, your loved one breaks down and cries.

- **Secondary Recipients – family and friends: store bought.** Family members and friends can quickly purchase value headsets.

- **Viewing.** Family and friends can join in this experience by watching it on their own headsets on Facebook. They may feel connected from a world away.

One last prayer with God. In our last hospice example, we look at creating a quiet experience for your loved one to pray to God from their favorite place.

Backstory. Your loved one has attended services every Sunday for years and they love their spiritual leader. In this 360 hospice personal experience (VR Prayer), your loved one would like to pray from their place of worship own one last time. Once again, your adult child helps to make this experience a reality with blazing speed.

360 Recipient

- **Primary Recipient:** Your loved one.
- **Secondary Recipients:** Your family and friends, who can join in praying to God.

360 Theme

- Last prayer with God from your loved one's place of worship.

360 Participants

- Only your adult child who will be silent.

360 Environment

- The front pew.

360 Experience

- **Point of view.** Your loved one feels as if they are in the front row of their place of worship.

- **Setup.** With permission from the spiritual leader, your adult child places the 360 camera on a tripod, puts it on the first pew, and raises it to eye level.

- **Recording and experience.** Your helper quietly presses start on the phone app while sitting next to the 360 camera. They say nothing for ten minutes.

- **Uploading.** After ten minutes, your adult child ends the recording and immediately uploads it to Facebook.

360 Delivery

- **Primary Recipient: professional delivery.** Your adult child goes to the hospice center. Once there, they deliver a headset to the nurse.

- **Viewing.** The nurse gently lays the headset on your loved one's head. Your loved one immediately realizes they are in their own special place of worship. Here, sitting in the front row, they begin to pray out loud as if from their own place of worship one more time.

They feel like they are in the first pew, praying for their family.

- **Secondary Recipients – family and friends: store bought.** Family members and friends can purchase headsets from a local store.

- **Viewing.** The family member or friend can place on the headset to join in the prayer for the primary recipient and their loved ones. They may be a world away, but they can feel connected with a new reality tool.

360 Community Experiences

Your virtual reality department can start creating your own local 360 community experiences. Here are four one-size-fits-all categories of 360 community experiences.

- **Meditative.**

  - Meditate at a local garden with a local pianist.
  - Be mindful from a local beach as the patient watches the sunset as a local singer gently sings a song.

- **Spiritual.**

  - Hear a holiday message from a local spiritual leader.
  - Listen to an encouraging message from a local spiritual leader.

- **Adventurous.**

  - Take a museum tour.
  - Skydive over the local community.

- **Motivational.**

  - Hear a motivational message from a patient that went

through the same experience.
- Hear an encouraging message from a local celebrity.

Virtual Reality Applications

Your department can search the best applications for your patients to watch. I recommend you watch and select the best and safest experiences beforehand. Many of these experiences may cause physical and emotional stress. Visit **www.vrformainstreet.com** for a list of top recommendations for you to showcase. Here is a brief list of examples:

- Join an African safari.
- Visit the Eiffel Tower.
- Watch a movie with their sibling on the moon.
- Play a fun video game.

Virtual Reality Stations

- **Private static stations.** Your facility may incorporate a private static station. This station may be its own room, a quiet place on a deck overlooking a lake, or a private place in your facility. Here a patient can view an immersive 360 personal experience, 360 community experience, or virtual reality application.

- **Public static stations.** This public static station should be in a safe place that is monitored for safety. This station can be utilized by patients and their loved ones visiting them. Hospice visits can be very emotional. This public station offers visitors the opportunity to pray from a local church or meditate on the beach. This may help their ability to support their hospice patient and other family members during this time.

- **Mobile static stations.** This mobile station can follow the patient around the hospice facility, if appropriate. For example, a patient would like to go outside at the hospice facility to feel the breeze as they virtually meditate on a local beach. Additionally, this mobile unit can be rolled or moved to bring to individual rooms in your facility.

Themed stations.

- **Superhero.** A children's hospice can create a themed room of a comic book superhero. The wall is painted with 3D imagery of the superhero flying through the sky. Also, the floor is painted 3D and gives the young child the illusion that they are in the clouds. The parent gently places on the headset. Instantly, the young child feels like they are flying through the skyscrapers of New York City as their favorite superhero.

- **Place of worship.** A senior, who has entered hospice care, has chosen to enter the spiritual-themed room. As the senior enters the room, they have the immediate feeling that they are in a spiritual place and feel peaceful. At this moment, a local spiritual leader asks what place of worship they attended. After hearing the answer, the spiritual leader nods their head and prepares the 360 video of that exact place of worship. The spiritual leader places on the headset. Immediately, the senior cries as they feel like they are in their place of worship.

Chapter 11: Summary

"Where would you like to go?" Your staff will be able to ask your patients this question once you have developed your virtual reality hospice department.

The hospital virtual reality hospice department may have the primary goal of patient satisfaction, assessed through patient surveys and key performance indicators.

Secondary goals may include public relations events and increased fundraising revenues.

Considerations for your hospice may include timeliness, support for patients with no support to make a 360 personal experience, viewing posting, emotional support, and the volume.

Chapter 11: Worksheet

Create your own virtual reality hospice department.

VR Hospice Department

Opportunities. What most excites you about a virtual reality last request?

_____

_____

_____

What training and support would you need to get started?

_____

_____

_____

360 Personal Experiences

What are three personal places you could have virtually brought patients in the past year?

_____

_____

_____

Visit loved ones. Where could you virtually bring your patients to feel connected with their loved ones and their favorite places in the community?

_____

_____

_____

Places to pray or mediate. Where could you virtually bring your patients to pray or meditate from their favorite places?

_____

_____

_____

360 Community Experiences

Pray. What community prayer experiences could you record for all future patients?

_____

_____

_____

_____

Meditate. What experiences could you record in your community to help your future patients to meditate or relax?

_____

_____

_____

Encouraging. What community experiences would help to encourage your patients?

_____

_____

_____

Adventure. Where would be some fun adventures for your patients to take in your community?

_____

_____

_____

Volunteers

Which local organizations can help you raise the money for VR headsets, cameras, and editing?

_____

_____

_____

Which local organizations can help create and deliver the experiences?

_____

_____

_____

Become More Competitive

Public relations. How can you showcase your 360 personal and community experiences to prospective clients?

_____

_____

_____

Fundraising. How could you leverage your 360 community experiences to raise money for your hospice?

_____

_____

_____

Chapter 12

Virtual Reality And Senior/Assisted Living

"The science of life is changing hearts and minds."

GARY BAUER

Do you wish you could virtually bring your residents to watch a local play or to spend time during the holidays with their family members who live across the country? We will look to solve this situation for your new department in Chapter 12. As you have learned thus far, when we embrace our new reality tool, we don't have to be in the same physical place to feel connected.

As a result, your facility can look at supporting your residents to feel more connected, loved, and empowered. Your new department can try to make this happen by helping your residents take a virtual trip to visit loved ones, a place in their community, or their own past to relive an old memory. You can accomplish this by creating a virtual reality department for your senior or assisted living facility.

In this chapter, we will explore the following topics:

- **Goals of your virtual reality department.**
- **Senior/assisted living considerations.**
- **Creating 360 personal experiences.**
- **Creating 360 community experiences.**
- **Virtual reality applications.**
- **How to use virtual reality stations.**

Goals Of Your Virtual Reality Department

Primary goals. The primary goals of your department will be to increase your patient satisfaction surveys and key performance indicators.

Secondary goals. As you learned in Chapters 10 and 11, your facility can look at creating a series of secondary goals. Let's look at two more for your senior/assisted living facility.

- **Improve happiness of residents.** You can look to create or improve your key performance indicators for happiness and wellbeing. These experiences may help your residents feel connected and loved, which, in turn, could make them happier and easier to care for, and allow them to have a better time connecting with other residents.

- **Volunteer organizations.** You can explore expanding support from local organizations, college students, high school students, and business associations.

- **Small projects.**

  - **Think small to start.** I suggest you start with a series of smaller projects to build the case for funding and support from your staff, residents, and community.

  - **What to measure.** As your residents initially watch your 360 personal and community experiences, your team may wish both to record and measure the results of these immersive videos. Here are only a few things to potentially measure:

    …Before and after physical evaluation (blood pressure, pulse, etc.)

…Before and after mental evaluation
…Before and after behavioral evaluation (anxiety levels)

Senior/Assisted Living Considerations

As you learned in the previous three chapters, you will need to address many questions before rolling out your initiatives. Here are a few more items to consider.

Be patient with yourself and others. Using virtual reality as a daily function in your facility will be new for everyone. Please be patient with yourself, your new team, your facility leaders, and your residents. To alleviate as much stress as possible, I recommend experimenting before you introduce this new connection tool to your residents. Hopefully, you will quickly learn that creating your own experiences is quite simple.

Clear expectations. Conceivably, your department's virtual reality trips will be overwhelmingly popular at your facility. I would lay out clear expectations of what your department can and cannot offer your residents.

Not designed to replace real human interaction. These immersive experiences are not meant to replace real human interaction. However, they may be radically superior to a phone call, video call, or greeting card.

Delivering the experience. I suggest you monitor your residents as they watch an immersive experience. This will help ensure they are safe from hurting themselves physically or emotionally.

- **Protection from physical movement.** Your residents may have a desire to swing their arms, swat something in the air, or grab something. This may cause them to accidentally hit another resident, knock something over, or bump into a chair.

This could result in an injury.

They may feel the need to physically walk around as they watch the experience. This could lead to an accidental trip or injury.

- **Post-viewing.** After viewing an experience, your resident may require an element of care that brings their mind and heart back to their real reality. As your resident switches from virtual reality to their real reality, they may need additional emotional support to calm down. This care can help them talk about their anxiety and isolation.

Prepare to be the expert. People in your community may look to you and your new department for help in starting their own virtual reality programs. You can decide to step up and be the virtual reality leader for your community or simply recommend they buy this book. Your colleagues can also visit **www.vrformainstreet.com** for more information.

> People in your community may look to you and your new department for help in starting their own virtual reality programs.

Sharing of headsets. You will need to determine your rules for cleanliness and use of headsets. I suggest each resident be assigned their own headset.

Now, let's jump in and learn the functions of your virtual reality department.

Creating 360 Personal Experiences

Creating 360 personal experiences allows your residents to

virtually travel to their own past, to the present, or to their projected future. Below are a few 360 themes to get you started down the right path. Visit Chapter 4 for a detailed explanation of the six steps in creating your own 360 personal experiences.

Present-day experiences. With these 360 personal experiences, your residents will feel like they are with their loved ones from a world away during their big (and small) events. Your residents can view these simple and everyday experiences hundreds of times throughout the year to feel connected. As they sit in their room alone or at a virtual reality station, they can simply put on their headset to take this immersive bridge to family and friends.

- **Birthday parties.** Your department can look to facilitate virtual trips where your residents can visit family and friends for their birthday parties. Most likely, your department will spend most of its time facilitating virtual parties for your residents.

- **Fourth of July.** Your virtual reality department can help facilitate a resident visiting their family during their Fourth of July celebration from a world away.

- **Peaceful time at the beach.** As a caregiver, you can virtually bring your resident on a trip to the local beach.

Past experiences. Virtual reality allows your residents to visit their pasts to help them build their faith, remember relationships, or reflect on their life victories.

- **First kiss.** You can help your resident take a virtual trip to their first kiss with their spouse.

- **First deployment.** Your department can record a 360 personal experience where a resident was first deployed to Vietnam. This was the exact place they remember from all those years ago.

- **Old business.** You can help a family member create an immersive video to your resident's past by allowing the senior to spend time in a walking tour of their old business back in Pennsylvania.

Creating 360 Community Experiences

The possibilities for your 360 community experiences are innumerable. These experiences will allow your residents to feel a part of your local community since they will virtually leave their real room and head out into the local community. These virtual excursions can bring your residents to a place to meditate, worship, have an adventure, or get motivated.

Meditation. Create meditation experiences for your residents to feel relaxed and to meditate from a beautiful place in your community. These calming local locations can include:

- Beaches.
- Parks.
- Gardens.
- Yoga or spiritual studios.
- Hiking trails.
- A place to watch the sunset.
- The snowy corner of your main street with a holiday bell ringer.

Your immersive experiences can include the calming background sounds of people in your community. Make sure you have permission to use these background sounds. Here are a few examples of creating calming sounds for your meditative 360 videos.

- Singers and bands.
- Choirs.

- Acoustical guitarists.
- Holiday bell ringers.

Spiritual. Your 360 community experiences may include connecting your residents with their local places of worship. Here are only a few opportunities for your department:

- Create holiday messages from local spiritual leaders near a holiday scene.
- Create an encouraging spiritual word for a resident who hasn't seen a visitor in quite a while.
- Create a loving message from a spiritual leader after a friend in assisted living has recently passed away.

Adventures. You can virtually bring your residents to an adventurous place in their community. With these experiences, you can create fun adventures for your residents to leave their rooms and become a part of the community again.

- **Friday night concerts.** Work with your local community center to create 360 videos of their Friday night concerts. Once completed, your residents can place on their headsets to feel like they are in the front row of a local concert.

- **Nature tours.** Your department can head out into nature to record tours for your residents. Here a few examples to consider for your new department.

  - Hiking trails.
  - Mountaintop sunsets.
  - Whale watching.

Motivation. Often, your residents can use a bit of motivation and a reminder that they are awesome. A reminder that they are not alone and are not forgotten. As your department unfolds, you can make a difference in your resident's life by virtually bringing them to a special place in your community to hear a motivational message from a local leader.

Virtual Reality Applications

Your new department can suggest several virtual reality applications to view. These simulations will allow your resident to fully interact in an immersive experience that allows them to play a game on Mars, solve a mystery game, watch a movie with their sibling on the beach, or relax on a Hawaiian beach. I would strongly suggest you review these simulations first to look for the following:

- Adult content.
- Violence.
- Messages of hate.
- Volume (too low or too high).
- Excessive movements.
- Lighting and flashing lights.

How To Use Virtual Reality Stations

Next, your department will need to support the proper delivery of your virtual reality experiences. By delivery, I mean your resident can properly and safely view your experiences.

Static stations: private. Your facility can consider a private static station that can be accessed privately and safely in your facility. Here a patient can relax in a quiet room to access your experiences with their standalone headset or by plugging in their own high-end headset.

Public stations.

- **Residents.** Your department can create a public station where your residents only need to plug in their high-end virtual reality headset to be immersed in another reality.

- **The resident's visitors.** Many times, the resident's family member or friend will require a safe place to virtually travel. In these times of stress or emotional pain, their visitors can visit a spiritual place to pray, surf in Oceanside California, or meditate on a mountaintop.

Mobile stations. A mobile station allows your caregivers the opportunity to bring top of the line virtual reality equipment into the room of a resident. Here, your resident can take a virtual trip during a tough emotional period or a time when they are in physical pain.

Themed Stations. Themed stations allow your residents to become completely immersed in a virtual reality theme. These themed rooms will need to be in their own space, which is easily accessed by your residents and monitored by your facility's staff.

- **Relaxing at sunset.** As your resident enters this room, they are immersed in an experience that helps them feel they have just traveled to visit a San Diego Beach. The walls and floors are painted with 3D imagery; the room smells like the ocean, and even sounds like the ocean since they hear the waves. Their feet feel the sand as they sit on a comfortable beach chair overlooking the ocean. At this exact moment, the caregiver places the headset on your resident. Instantly, the resident feels like they just flew to San Diego to relax on the beach.

- **Hiking room.** Your resident wants to take a virtual hiking trip through a local trail. As they enter the room, they will view the 3D paintings on the wall and floor that put them in the middle of a nature trail. The room smells and even sounds like nature. A virtual reality headset, attached to the ceiling, dangles in the middle of the room. Next, the nurse places this high-end headset on the resident. Immediately, they feel like they are walking on a local hiking trail with a park ranger giving the tour.

Chapter 12: Summary

The primary goals of your department may be to increase your patient satisfaction surveys and key performance indicators.

Secondary goals could be to improve resident happiness, increase support from volunteers, increase fundraising revenues, and start smaller projects.

You will need to be patient with yourself, your staff, the residents, and the residents' families.

Your department should consider laying out clear expectations because your residents may line up to take their virtual trips.

Consider reaching out to local colleges for volunteer support.

Your new department is not supposed to replace human interaction.

Prepare to be the expert in your community.

Chapter 12: Worksheet

Here are a few questions to help you start developing your virtual reality senior/assisted living department.

Getting Started

What are you most excited about with this new department?

_____

_____

_____

What planning and training areas will you need support in?

_____

_____

_____

What research do you need before you begin?

_____

_____

_____

360 Personal Experiences

Would you hire new staff? Or would you choose to outsource the activities to volunteers?

_____

360 Community Experience

What community locations would you record?

_____

_____

_____

Why them?

_____

_____

_____

Community Support

Who in the community would support your department?

_____

_____

_____

Public Relations And Advertising

How could you use your new department in your public relations campaign?

_____

_____

_____

How could you leverage these new connections to become more competitive?

_____

_____

_____

How could you incorporate a VR mobile station with your community relations and media interviews?

_____

_____

_____

PART FOUR

Virtual Reality In Your Marketing
Communications

Chapter 13
Virtual Reality In Public Relations

"What made the difference was the vision of how things could be and clearly painting the picture for all to see and comprehend."

MARK D'ARCANGELO

In such a loud world, are you looking to breakthrough with a message that deeply connects with your targeted audience? Then, you should consider utilizing virtual reality to tell your story. Virtual reality allows your audience to enter your experience as if they were with you in your messaging. This idea is radically different than watching a TV commercial. Your target audience will feel like they are in the story. In fact, they may feel like they, rather than a Hollywood supermodel, are the star of the message.

Our new reality tool allows you to send an immersive bridge to bring your targeted audience to wherever you would like to virtually bring them. So the real question is, "Where would you like to take them?" We will answer that question in this chapter.

Here is what you will learn in Chapter 13:

- **Connect with your 360 recipients (target audience).**
- **Where you are virtually taking your 360 recipients.**
- **Internal public relations campaigns.**
- **External public relations campaigns.**

Connect With Your 360 Recipients (target audience)

This chapter's intention is only to start this conversation with you. In doing so, it's my goal to keep it simple by consistently utilizing 360 personal and community experiences. At this point, there's no need to overcomplicate this topic. Let's jump in and take a high level look at incorporating virtual reality into your public relations campaigns.

Primary recipients. As with any plan, you will need to clearly identify your target audience. Earlier, in Chapter 4, I described this as the primary recipient of your 360 videos.

> The primary recipient(s) is the person (or group of people) for whom the video is created.

To be consistent, I will continue to call your target audience(s) the primary recipients. Therefore, your primary recipients may include your customers, prospects, shareholders, media, and the community. As they put on their headset, the primary recipient will know that the immersive experience was created for them.

> Your primary recipients may include your customers, prospects, shareholders, media, and the community.

Secondary recipients. You can create experiences where someone can virtually walk in the shoes of another person or group of people. This will allow the viewer of your experience to create empathy for a person (or group of people). In other words, when the secondary recipient dons the headset, they will instantly know that this video was not created for them. They will continue to watch the experience from the primary recipient's point of view. This will help the secondary recipient understand the viewpoint of the primary recipient. Here's how I defined this recipient in Chapter 4.

A secondary recipient is a person who views the 360 personal experience through the eyes of another. This immersive video gives secondary recipients special access into the lives of the primary recipient(s). Ultimately, the video allows the secondary recipient to virtually walk in the primary recipient's point of view to build empathy and better understand their past, present, and projected future.

Where You Are Virtually Sending Your Recipients

In creating your public relations campaign, your business can virtually bring your primary and secondary recipients to the past, the present, or the future.

Today's recording of reenacting the past. Your public relations team can reenact an important event from your business's past. In this experience, the primary and secondary participants will feel like they are in the video of an old memory of the past. This is not a video they are watching on their phone.

They will feel like they have entered a portal to the past.

Retirement example.

- **360 Personal Experience.** You can create this experience for your parent as they retire from your family's business. Your parent is passing the family business on to you and you would like to virtually bring them personally back to the house that you grew up in. In this 360 personal experience, you and your family can thank your parent for their hard work and the family values they have passed on to you. In this experience, your family, the mayor, and your top customers will say thank you in a heartfelt message as everyone walks through your former home.

In this example, the parent is the primary recipient. As they place on their headset, your parent will instantly know that this experience was made for them personally. With this mind, this 360 personal experience can be a private experience for only the family to view. Or this experience can be used as a public relations tool to be shared with the community. In this instance, community members would be the secondary recipients. They will participate in this virtual reality walking tour and feel a part of such an emotional message from the heart.

- **360 Community Experience.** Let's use the same example and turn it around to become a 360 community experience. Here, the primary recipients will be the whole community. The immersive bridge will take the community on a walking tour of the home you grew up in. In this 360 video, the community will hear you and your parent talk about how your family business started and how you both are so proud to be part of the local community.

At the end of the video, the community will take a seat at your kitchen table in an open chair experience. Here, a local resident will feel like they are sitting at the table to hear the personal story of how this business became such an important part of the community. In a sense, a local resident will feel a part of the business's family.

Past events example. Your business can create a 360 community experience that virtually brings the community back to its past. In this public relations example, your business could work with your local historical society to reenact important events in your community's past. In doing so, your business can convey the message that your business has been a staple of your community's downtown for more than 100 years.

Today's recordings to be viewed in the future. Your business can create 360 videos of events today in your business or community. The intention of these immersive videos is for your primary and secondary recipients to enjoy these 360 videos for decades to come. Let's look at one example.

- **Future-orientated example.** Your business can begin creating virtual reality (360) recordings of your community events to be viewed in the future. For example, you can record your downtown holiday lights to be viewed for decades to come. This isn't a video on your phone. This is an immersive bridge to your community's past.

- **Mission of Virtual Reality for Main Street movement.** As we move into our new industrial age, it is conceivable that our local downtowns will disappear and never return. An old picture of a downtown is always fun to look at on a local brewery's wall. But imagine if you could put on a virtual reality headset and feel like you are walking downtown from twenty years ago. Preserving your downtown's memory is a mission of the Virtual Reality for Main Street Movement. Contact me at **www.info@vrformainstreet.com** to preserve your community's history.

Today's recording of a possible future. As you learned in Chapter 7, you can create immersive bridges for people to feel like they are living in the future. Imagine people in your community being able to place on your headsets and view the vision of your company's building project. In this example, a local resident can see the finished project in a virtual reality walking tour. For this type of public relations campaign, you will need to create a virtual reality application that will allow you to present a computer-generated version of the future. Contact me for more information on creating a future virtual reality simulation of your project's completion (**info@vrformainstreet.com**).

How to add virtual reality to your public relations campaigns. Now, let's start bringing this all together by learning how to create your own internal and external public relations campaigns.

Internal Public Relations Campaigns

As you have learned throughout this book, virtual reality is more than a great way to play a video game. You now have the tools to create empathetic experiences where you can gather support for your internal public relations activities. It's more than watching a video on your Facebook page. Let's look at how you can create immersive videos to unleash your ability to connect with your primary recipients (target audiences).

Missions/values. As a leader, I assume you have attempted to rally your team to a new mission and to present your core values. These initiatives may have gone well, or they never materialized through your organization. What if you could paint a better picture of your initiatives by creating a virtual reality story of why this is important to your staff? This is not another traditional video. It might be a thought-provoking and inspiring immersive experience where your team will feel connected to the mission.

Think of it this way: You are not creating another collateral piece or a cool logo. You are creating a virtual reality experience where your staff will gain empathy for you and for your vision by having them feel like they are in the story—not just watching a video on their phone. Let's look at an example to help you put your head around the concept.

New VIP segment example. With so much change, you and your executive team embrace machine learning to better understand your customers' segmentation. In this analysis, you clearly see that your top segments have changed in the last few years. You will need to revise parts of your mission statement to address this shift and adapt to your top segments.

This new initiative is much deeper and mission-driven to help create longer term relationships with your emerging audience. The mission will focus on connecting with your wellness and environmentally conscious customers.

Backstory. You are creating a public relations 360 community experience for your employees to embrace your new mission and to better understand the business's top new customer segment. In doing so, your company's new mission is to protect the local nature preserve and its habitat. Your company is committed to preserving this area because it gives local residents a chance to connect with nature.

360 Recipients

- **Primary Recipients:** Your employees.
- **Secondary Recipients:** Target audience.

  - Your target audience (secondary recipients) will be presented these 360 videos to watch on your Facebook page. They will gain empathy with your new mission statement and will form a deeper connection with your brand.

This secondary audience is women, who are 25-54, college educated, married, love the outdoors, wellness orientated, and concerned about the environment.

- **Shareholders.** Your shareholders will view the experience as secondary recipients as they learn how you are connecting with company employees and your target audience in a new and innovative manner.

- **Media.** The media will be presented with this virtual reality experience to showcase your company's shift to becoming a community leader by taking care of the local environment. This video can be used by the local media to showcase the nature preserve and hear from local experts why this area is so important to keep clean, free, and available to everyone.

360 Theme

- The theme of the public relations video is to rally your employees around your new company mission of being a community leader in the outdoors and nature preserve.

- **Note:** I chose a simple experience to get started. You may need to spend more time in planning your 360 video.

360 Participants

- You (the CEO), your executive team, the local mayor, and an environmental expert.

360 Environment

- A tour of the local nature preserve.

360 Experience

- **Point of view.** Your employees will enter the immersive experience by feeling like they are walking with you on a tour of a local nature preserve.

- **Setup.** One of your employees acts as the camera person by simply placing a 360 camera on a head strap (or helmet). This person will walk with you throughout the tour.

- **Recording.** When you're ready, you hit start on your phone's camera app. Next, you look into the 360 camera as if it were your primary recipient's. In this conversation, your 360 participants can discuss the following:

  - Introduce the preserve.
  - Explain your mission.
  - Let the mayor explain the history.
  - A local expert can talk about the monthly activities.

- **Editing.** Hire a local video editing company to properly edit the video.

- **Uploading.** Upload the video to your website and social media sites.

360 Delivery

- **Primary Recipients – employee conference.** At the next employee conference, you deliver the experience by placing a headset under each chair. At the perfect moment, you ask everyone to grab their headset and then proceed to teach them how to view your experience.

- **Viewing.** Instruct your employees to watch your immersive video at another time during the conference.

- **Secondary Recipients – target audience: store pickup.** Your targeted audience will need to purchase their own headsets.

- **Viewing.** This target audience will view your team on Facebook with their sleeves rolled and taking massive action at the nature preserve.

- **Secondary Recipients – shareholders: mailed.** Your shareholders will receive a care package from you that may include a standalone headset, instructions on how to view the experience, and information about your new mission.

- **Note:** A standalone headset is a virtual reality headset that doesn't require your phone or a cord connecting it to a gaming computer. This headset costs $199.

- **Viewing.** Your shareholders will watch your immersive video from their living room with a top-rated headset. This will help them understand your new mission and how your leadership quickly adapts to our changing world.

- **Secondary Recipients – media: mailed.** You can create a care package for your local television/radio stations and social media influencers. This package could contain a press release, standalone virtual reality headset, link to the Facebook video, and instructions on how to view the experience.

- **Viewing.** The media outlet (or personality) will watch the immersive video and may feel connected to your new mission. Afterwards, they may feel moved and inspired to share your newsworthy story with their listeners/readers.

- **Shareholder meeting.** You can now add empathic virtual reality experiences to your next shareholder's meeting or conference.

This new video format will allow your shareholders to take a virtual trip to learn about new projects, new research, and even a new way to present data. This is not another video to watch on a big screen.

They will feel like they are with you and your team from a world away.

New warehouse example. There has been some confusion about the status of a new warehouse. This facility is in another state, and you would like to address this confusion at the next shareholder's meeting.

Backstory. There have been a few hiccups along the way, but your new warehouse is nearing completion and will be completed on time.

360 Recipients

- **Primary Recipients:** Your company's shareholders.
- **Secondary Recipients:** None. This is a private and secure experience.

360 Theme

- This will be a simple walking tour of the facility.

360 Participants

- You (the CEO), the warehouse manager, and a small team of warehouse employees.

360 Environment

- A tour of the warehouse.

360 Experience

- **Point of view.** It's one thing to read a report or watch a traditional video. It's something entirely different when your shareholders view a virtual tour of your new warehouse's progress.

- **Setup.** Place the 360 camera on the top of an employee's head strap (or helmet).

- **Recording.** When you're ready, you will walk through your facility and talk to the 360 camera as if it were a shareholder.

- **Editing.** You can edit this video or keep it raw. This is a simple walking tour.

- **Uploading.** Upload the 360 video as a private link on your company's YouTube channel.

- **Note:** This could be a live experience where the 360 recipients and participants can talk with each other over your phone's speaker.

360 Delivery

- **Mailed.** Your team will mail out a personal care package to each shareholder. This package will include a headset, paperwork on the warehouse's status, and instructions on how to watch the private video on YouTube.

- **Viewing.** Once they place on their headsets, the shareholders will see for themselves the 360 status of the warehouse.

- **Internal market segments.** With virtual reality, you can pick your market segment and create a story of their daily lives. This would not be for public consumption.

This would only be used internally to help your employees gain empathy and better understand your top market segment(s). As an employee dons the headset, they will view the experience as a secondary recipient and witness a 360 personal experience of a day in the life of your primary recipients (target audience). Let's look at an example.

New VIP segment example. Virtual reality allows you to create immersive stories about your top marketing segments. This can be a powerful tool because it will teach your executives, salespeople, and customer service staff to have a deep understanding and appreciation for your top segments.

Backstory. You would like your team to increase customer service performance. You have a new competitor that is aggressively targeting your client base. One way to combat this is with breathtaking customer service. Your competitor is selling price. Your company has always focused on delivering value and the best customer service in your market.

To add to this strong customer success reputation, you decide to teach your entire staff who your top market segment is and to create empathy for them.

360 Recipients

- **Primary Recipients:** None. No primary recipients (the target audience) will watch this experience.
- **Secondary Recipients:** In this example, this immersive experience is a day in the life of Ashley. Ashley is a fictitious person who fits your target audience perfectly. She is a local working mother of three young children. Your staff will live a day through Ashley's "eyes."

360 Theme

- The theme will be a story of your target audience (Ashley). Your employees can live a day in their top customers' shoes to better understand who they are and what's important to them. Think of this experience as creating your target customer as a comic book hero.

360 Participants

- A local family that fits your top market profile. This family will include a spouse and three children. The 360 participants will talk to "Ashley" as if she were there in person. But she is not present in the video as your staff will enter the experience as "Ashley."

360 Environment

- Your employees will enter the 360 environment from the viewpoint of the mother of a local family. This edited immersive video will have three environments:

  1. The kitchen table during the family breakfast.
  2. The mother's office during the day.
  3. The family living room before the television in the evening.

360 Experience

- **Point of view.** Your employees will enter the experience as living a day in the life of your target demographic.

- **Setup.** Secure your 360 camera on the mother's head through a helmet cam or helmet straps.

- **Recording.** When everyone is ready, hit start on your phone's camera app (via Bluetooth) and record the three scenarios (breakfast, work, end of day).

- **Editing.** You will need to hire a local editor to edit the many different 360 video captures throughout the day.

- **Note:** I would recommend adding text on the bottom of the edited video to support any staff members who are hearing impaired or deaf.

- **Uploading.** Only upload your video to a private YouTube channel.

360 Delivery

- **Primary Recipients.** None

- **Secondary Recipients – employee conference.** At your next employee conference, you will place a value headset under each seat (with your company logo). At the appropriate time, one of your executive team members or a virtual reality specialist will ask your employees to grab their headsets and give a detailed explanation on how to view the experience.

  Additionally, you can create a collateral piece with a detailed written story of your comic book hero (your target demographic) and instructions on how to view the immersive video. Due to the chaos of hundreds of people trying something for the first time, I would recommend your employees' attempt to view the virtual reality video at another time.

- **Viewing.** Your employees will watch the video later during the conference in their small group sessions or on their own personal time.

External Public Relations Campaigns

Next, let's turn our attention to creating a strong brand by unleashing your ability to tell your company's story to the community. As you have learned throughout this book, your company is now forced to compete with quantum computers, artificial intelligence, robotics, and advances in online personalization. Moreover, with the emergence of 5G, your business will be thrust into a world of four new realities.

My intention in this next section is to help you think about bringing people the tools of the next era in a way that will inspire your community to embrace upcoming changes. In doing so, you are a true leader in your community. You are leading the way by showing your community not only how to exist in our new era, but how to thrive in its potential to unleash our ability to connect with others.

Let's explore a few 360 themes to help explore this topic.

Company causes. Many consumers are looking for their favorite brands to champion the causes important to them. From this starting point, you can now create immersive public relations messages that virtually bring your target audience into the actions you are taking in your company cause. Your target audience doesn't have to read your website or watch another vulnerable message on Facebook. Your target audience gets to see what your company is doing and how they are moving the cause forward.

F* cancer example.** In this example, we will look at the devastation of cancer in your community. As a leader in your business and community, you have experienced the destruction of cancer in your employees and family's lives over the past few decades. In an epiphany, you decide you can create some of the most loving and memorable experiences for people in your community experiencing difficult times. This isn't about a new sound bite or a cool Facebook video.

You are tired of this ailment, and you are committed to being there for the people in your community. No one in your community ever has to feel alone in the hospital room ever again.

Backstory. As a leader, you have seen the trauma and depression a person experiences in their cancer struggle. You decide to create 360 community experiences for patients to enjoy in these horrific times. In doing so, you brand your company as humanitarian and a thought leader by using our new reality tools for the good of the people in your community.

- **Secondary Recipients**

  - **Target audiences.** These moving community experiences will connect with your targeted audience because you are doing something in your community. Other companies may be utilizing quantum computers, but your business is committed to making a difference.

  - **Media.** The media in your community will see this for what it is. A way to deploy our new reality tools to help the people in your community. This news story will have legs for years because the reporter could discuss virtual reality as caring, changing people's lives, and becoming a thought leader for innovation.

  - **Shareholders.** Shareholders will be moved by your ability to embrace change to deeply connect with your community. This view of you will pay dividends as we all move into our new world.

  - **New capital investors.** Investors may watch these 360 community experiences and feel excited about your company's ambition to stay relevant in a world of hyper-innovation and hyper-connection.

- **Attracting talent.** These inspiring public relations initiatives will attract the talent in your community. The initiatives will set you apart because talented people will see how you will survive the upcoming tsunami of change.

360 Theme

- Experiences of hope, love, and support during difficult times. The primary recipient will feel like they are on a hike with you (the CEO). Here, the primary recipient will hear your story of how cancer has affected you personally and learn that you are committed to ensuring they are not alone.

  As you move up the trail, you come to a sunset where your whole team is at the top of the trail overlooking the ocean.

  It is here that people start holding up signs and walking up to the camera (the POV of the patient) to say they are not alone, and the cancer patient is loved!

360 Participants

- **Beginning.** The first part of the experience is where the cancer patient is walking up the trail with you (the CEO).

- **Trailhead.** A few minutes later, you arrive at the trailhead with the ocean in the background. At this point, your preselected employees hold up signs and give a very brief word of encouragement.

360 Environment

- For this example, we will virtually bring a cancer patient to a local hiking trail to feel moved and inspired.

360 Experience

- **Point of view.** The cancer patient will feel like they are walking up a hiking trail with you.

- **Setup.** You place a 360 camera on top of the helmet of one of your employees. Your employee will walk next to you as your cameraperson. Their only job is to walk near you.

- **Recording.**

  - **Beginning.** You begin the immersive video by walking up the hiking trail. As you proceed, you open up your heart to share how cancer has affected your family and employees. You make a commitment that cancer sufferers and their families don't have to do this alone.

  - **Trailhead.** You and the cancer patient arrive at the trailhead to view your fifty employees. Here, your staff is holding up signs of encouragement and telling the patient they are not alone; the whole community loves them!

  - **Note:** Avoid areas of excessive sunlight.

- **Editing.** You will need to hire a local professional to edit this video.

- **Uploading.**

  - **Virtual reality department – private.** First upload this video to the hospital's computer at the virtual reality station. That way, the experience can remain private and only be viewed by an actual cancer patient during a hospital stay.

  - **Social media – public.** This video can be uploaded to your social media.

360 Delivery

- **Hospital patient: virtual reality department**. Work with your hospital's virtual reality department to upload the 360 video to their virtual reality station.

- **Viewing.** With the doctor's permission, the patient will place on the high-end headset to take the virtual trip to hear your company's message of hope.

- **Media: mailed.** You can send a care package to your favorite media outlets. The package could include a standalone headset, instructions on how to view the experience, hospital contact information, and information on the possibilities of virtual reality and the care of patients.

- **Viewing.** The reporter will watch the experience. Afterwards, they may want to interview the local doctor on how the experience worked in the hospital environment.

- **Shareholders: mailed.** As you learned earlier in this chapter, you can send your shareholders a care package that could include a standalone headset, instructions on how to view the video, and a note from the patient for investing in your company.

- **Viewing.** Your shareholders will receive the care package and be moved by your ability to deeply connect and inspire the local community.

Chapter 13: Summary

The primary recipient(s) is the person (or group of people) for whom the video is created.

- Your public relations target audience is your primary recipients.

- A secondary recipient is a person who views the 360 personal experience through the eyes of another. This immersive video gives secondary recipients special access into the lives of the primary recipient(s).

Ultimately, the video allows the secondary recipient to virtually walk in the primary recipient's point of view to build empathy and better understand their past, present, and projected future.

In public relations, your secondary recipients may include your shareholders, the people in your community, or the media.

- You can create today's recording of reenacting the past.
- You can create todays' recording for the future.

A mission of the Virtual Reality Movement is to preserve downtowns by recording them for future usage. Imagine placing on a headset and feeling like you're walking downtown from twenty years ago.

- You can record today's recording of a possible future.
- 360 videos allow you to deeply connect with your internal audiences: shareholders, staff, and the media.
- You can embrace virtual reality to start a new, deep connection with your external audiences.

Chapter 13: Worksheet

Create your own virtual reality public relations campaign.

360 Recipients

Primary Recipient(s) (Target Audience): Who are your primary recipients?

_____

_____

_____

Is there more than one primary recipient?

_____

_____

_____

Secondary Recipients: Who else will watch your experience?

_____

_____

_____

How will this immersive experience create empathy for your primary recipients (target audience)?

_____

_____

_____

How will your secondary recipients be moved and inspired by your 360 videos?

_____

_____

_____

360 Themes

What would be the theme (purpose)?

_____

_____

_____

How will this messaging connect with your target audience?

_____

_____

_____

360 Participants

Who should be in the video recording?

_____

_____

_____

What would they say to encourage or inspire your primary and secondary recipients?

_____

_____

_____

360 Environment

Where would you like to bring your primary and secondary recipients?

_____

_____

_____

Would you virtually bring them to the past, present, or future?

_____

_____

Why bring them there?

_____

_____

_____

How will this experience help your customers connect with your company's mission?

_____

_____

_____

360 Experience

What would you like the experience to look like?

_____

_____

_____

Where would you upload the experience?

_____

_____

_____

What permissions will you need?

_____

_____

_____

Will this experience be live or recorded?

_____

_____

_____

Will this experience be private or public?

_____

_____

_____

360 Delivery

How would you like to deliver your experiences to your VIPs?

_____

_____

_____

The media?

_____

_____

_____

To shareholders?

_____

_____

_____

What would you include in your care package that the headset is mailed?

_____

_____

_____

Chapter 14
Virtual Reality And Advertising

"There's decades of innovations ahead. We're at the very beginning, where it's just at the stage where we can bring in consumers [but] there's so much further to go from there."

B R E N D A N   I R I B E

Are you looking to break through all the noise of traditional and digital advertising? Then it might be time to consider embracing virtual reality in your advertising mix. This new medium allows you to create an immersive bridge that allows your primary recipient (target audience) to take a virtual trip to a place that is familiar to them (360 environment). The topic of virtual reality and advertising is worthy of another book. At this point, I would like to offer you a glimpse into what is possible by adding virtual reality to your advertising mix.

In this chapter, you will learn about:

- **New rules of advertising.**
- **360 personal experiences (advertising message).**

New Rules Of Advertising

Our new industrial age allows your business to form deeper connections with your target audiences (360 recipients). Here are three rules of our new era.

1. Personalization. With the tools of artificial intelligence, your business can now create highly personalized customer/prospect segments. This will allow your business to deploy pertinent and timely advertising messages.

- **Data science.** Data science allows your business up to the minute data from a multitude of sources. Here's a quick look at how they may gather that data:

  - What pages your customers visited on your website.
  - Current and past purchases.
  - How customers use social media.

- **Customer profiles.** Once you have received this data, you can articulate a points system in your content management system (CMS) to create customer profiles. These profiles are called personas, psychological profiles, and avatars. Once you have created your profiles, you can create different online experiences for each customer profile. For example, each profile will view a different home page on your website. Think of it as a personal experience through your brand's website. Your website will deeply understand each profile and offer timely and pertinent information.

- **Personalization example.** Your business can create a hyper-personalized campaign. In other words, your data science tools can offer personalized messages in a manner that is very personal to an individual user. For example, a shopper purchases a black pair of shoes on your company's website. Later in the week, your CMS has determined that this shopper is driving near your offline retail store.

Next, your CMS can automatically send a text message to that specific customer informing them that they can get a 10 percent off coupon for a black belt to match the black shoes.

2. Unleashed connection. With our new reality tools, we are moving into an era of hyper-connection that will unleash our ability to feel connected with our loved ones and the world around us. You may be excited about the possibilities of driverless cars. I personally get excited about our new ability to help connect family members in times of joy and difficulty.

3. Innovation. Product and business life cycles may be become much shorter as we move into an era of hyper-innovation.

360 personal experiences. As you move through this chapter, you will see an extension of the six steps we studied in Chapters 4 and 8. Why overcomplicate virtual reality? It is my intention to start this conversation with you in the simplest manner possible. For now, let's keep things simple to get started by thinking of virtual reality advertising as sending a 360 personal experience.

360 personal experiences are created for the purpose of sending out an immersive bridge for the primary recipient(s) to join you where you are in the present, to their past, or to their own projected future. To evaluate this topic, I will help you look at creating a basic and personalized advertising message.

Let's look at a basic virtual reality advertising message to start you in the right direction.

Fiftieth anniversary celebration example. Your furniture store has made it to the coveted fifty-year mark. In this journey, you have come so far and are grateful for the hundreds of people who have helped you along the way. This basic 360 video will allow you to virtually invite the community to share with you on your big celebration.

With virtual reality, you're not creating another coupon in the paper or a cool new logo.

You are creating an inspirational experience that you, your employees, and your community will cherish for years to come.

Backstory. During your fifty-year anniversary week, you decide to invite your customers and the community down memory lane.

360 Recipients

- **Primary Recipients:** Your customers, employees, shareholders, and the whole community.
- **Secondary Recipients: Media.** You and your team can turn this into an opportunity for the media to showcase your 360 video to their viewers as well.

360 Theme

- This will be a twelve-minute video that celebrates your fifty-year anniversary.

360 Participants

- **First location.** You and your family share the stories of how the business started with your parents fifty years ago this week.

- **Store.** The second part of the edited video will virtually bring the people in your community to your current furniture store. This part of the experience will allow your employees to share with the community how much they have enjoyed working with so many families through the decades.

360 Environment

- **First location.** The beginning of the video will virtually bring the community to the first location of your business fifty years ago. The building is still around but unused now.

- **Store.** At the store, you gather everyone in a circle around the 360 camera.

360 Experience

- **Point of view.** The community will enter your immersive bridge to both the first location and then to the store.

- **Setup.**

  - **First location.** Place your 360 camera on an employee's helmet. The employee will walk with you as you give a moving story of how your family started this business fifty years ago.

  - **Store.** Place chairs in a circle surrounding the 360 camera in the perfect spot at your store.

- **Recording.**

  - **First location**. Hit start and begin giving a walking tour of your family's first location.

  - **Store.** Have everyone sit down in their preassigned seats. As you begin, each preselected person will give their message of gratitude to the community.

- **Editing.** You may need to hire a local professional to edit this video.

- **Uploading.**

  - **Social media.** Your edited video can be uploaded to your social media.

- **Note:** Be aware of the size of your file to ensure social media can properly upload the video.

360 Delivery

- **Store pickup.** The community will need to purchase their own headsets.

- **Viewing.** The community will watch the experiences on your Facebook and YouTube channels.

Media mailed. You will need to mail a care package to favorite media outlets. In this package, you can include old newspaper clippings, copies of old photos, your press release, a standalone headset, and instructions on how to view the video.

Viewing. As people watch the 360 video, they will be virtually transported to the first location and will appreciate your virtual reality experiences. The media will share these experiences to their listeners/readers with the URL link you have sent them.

360 Personal Experiences (advertising message)

Now that we have learned how to create a basic virtual reality (360) video, let's move to a much more complicated campaign that utilizes 360 personal experiences in a personalized advertisement campaign.

Nine-month pregnancy. With a top-rated content management system (CMS), you can create hyper-personalized campaigns for your targeted customers. With this technology, your website can deploy messaging to the exact stage of your customer's pregnancy. For example, month two of the pregnancy, the expecting mother will see a completely different website homepage and product suggestions.

This will allow your business to form a deep connection with your customer because the customer will begin to see you as a valued partner that really understands them.

In taking this to another level, you can create a 360 personal experience to help the expecting mother during this important second month.

Backstory. A woman has entered the second month of pregnancy. She logs in to your website to view a whole new website geared to her second month. On this page, she will notice a 360 video for her to watch about her upcoming second month.

360 Recipients

- **Primary Recipients (target audience):** All expecting mothers in the start of their second month.
- **Secondary Recipients:** None.

360 Theme

- A video of what to expect in month two.

360 Participants

- This experience will only showcase a nationally recognized author and TV host.

360 Environment

- A well-lit living room near the company headquarters.

360 Experience

- **Point of view.** The expecting mother will enter your experience as sitting down on the comfortable couch in a conversation with the TV host.

- **Setup.** Have the TV host sit down next to the open chair where the primary recipient will enter your experience.

- **Recording.** Set up the 360 camera on a tripod on the open chair near the TV host. Then raise the tripod to eye-level with the TV host. That's it. Hit start when you're ready. The recording will offer pertinent and timely information about the mother's second month. Each woman may feel this 360 video was made personally for them.

- **Editing.** This video will need to be edited by a local professional.

- **Note:** I suggest you edit in a product offering at the end of the edited 360 video that would be a perfect fit for an expecting mother in the start of her second month. The video will also need to have a link to learn more.

- **Uploading.**

  - **Social media.** Upload your immersive video to your sites.

  - **CMS.** After you upload the video to YouTube, you can insert the URL of the video into your CMS to continue the personalization process.

360 Delivery

- **The expecting mother: store pickup.** The expecting mother will need to purchase her own headset.

- **Viewing: website.** You can feature this immersive video on your month two version of you hyper-personalized home page.

- **Social media.** You can create a video for each of the nine months and place them on your social media sites in succession.

- **Media: mailed.** You will need to mail a care package to favorite media outlets. In this package, you could send a standalone headset, instructions on how to view this personalized video, and a press release of your hyper-personalized advertising campaign.

- **Out to their listeners.** A few days later, they will watch your experience from their business. Quickly, they will understand how this is not a one-size-fits-all advertisement. This personalized video will make a real difference for the expecting mother.

- **Affiliates, bloggers, and influencers: mailed.** You can send your marketing affiliates a care package that includes a headset, new affiliate benefits, and new banner ads.

- **Note:** Affiliates are companies that promote your products and services for a fee.

- **Promotion.** After viewing the hyper-personalized advertisement, your top affiliates, bloggers, and influencers can quickly start promoting your new campaign.

Chapter 14: Summary

There are three new advertising rules in our new era:

1. Personalization.
2. Data Science.
3. Customer profiles.

Personalization allows your business to create personalized segments for marketing.

Data science tracks your customers' visits to your site, their purchases, and how they use social media.

Customer profiles have been called personality profiles, personas, and avatars.

CMS (content management system) allows your business to personalize your advertising campaigns.

Chapter 14: Worksheet

360 Recipients

Primary Recipient(s) (Target Audience): Who is your primary recipient(s)?

_____

_____

_____

Is there more than one primary recipient?

_____

_____

_____

Secondary Recipients: Who else will watch your experience?

_____

_____

_____

How will this immersive experience create empathy for your primary recipients (target audience)?

_____

_____

_____

How will your secondary recipients be emotionally moved by your 360 video?

_____

_____

_____

_____

360 Themes

What would be the theme (purpose)?

_____

_____

_____

360 Participants

Who should be in the video recording?

_____

_____

_____

What would they say to encourage or inspire your primary and secondary recipients?

_____

_____

_____

Would they be models, real customers, or actual employees?

_____

_____

_____

360 Environment

Where would you like to bring your primary recipient(s)?

_____

_____

_____

Would this environment be in the past, present, or future?

_____

_____

_____

360 Experience

Where would you upload the experience?

_____

_____

_____

Will it be live or recorded?

_____

Will it be a private (need a link) or public experience (social media, website)?

_____

_____

_____

360 Delivery

What would be the best headset for the primary recipients (target audiences) to view your experience?

_____

_____

_____

What would you include in your care package to VIP customers and the local media?

_____

_____

_____

A Final Word
Let's Get Started

I'm honored to have spent this time with you. I'm thrilled for the opportunities this book may have opened for you, your loved ones, your community, and your business. Our world is changing at a ferocious pace. But I believe we were made in the image of God and that humanity will learn to thrive in our new era.

It's up to all of us to bring the new tools of our generation into our world for the good of us all.

As you have learned, this next era is not only about a faster computer, a better way to play a video game, or having our cars drive us to work. It's also about giving you and your community the ability to form deep connections in our new realities.

In our new era, we don't have to be in the same physical place to feel connected any longer.

I wrote this book to be a call to action. The book's six steps and examples were designed to show you what's possible in an easy-to-read format. Now it's your turn. It's your turn to embrace technology to unleash you and your community's ability to connect with each other and to the world.

My final words will include the first step, a list of your next steps, an overview of each chapter, and how I can continue to support you in your initiatives.

First Step

The first step is to realize our next industrial era has arrived. This book was intended to help you and your community lead from the front and with your hearts. The rules of today and the past may not bear much weight as we move forward. We will most likely need to think of new solutions from a different perspective—a perspective that embraces our new technological tools.

Next Steps

Why read this book and take no action? Here are five action steps to get started on to make an impact in your community.

1. Learn the six steps of creating a 360 personal and community experience.
2. Purchase your first 360 camera.
3. Create your first 360 personal or community experience.
4. Share your experience on Facebook and your new YouTube channel.
5. Personally delivery your experience to someone in need.

Book Summary

This book was intended to start a conversation about getting you engaged in the "real game of our generation." This high-level content was designed to open your mind up to the possibilities of embracing our new reality tool called virtual reality.

At first glance, you may think this book has been about creating emotional and nature videos. It's much more than that. The book's content was created to take a very complex topic and break it down into easy-to-follow steps to bring everyone closer to using this new empathy tool. This book's goal was to demystify virtual reality and help prepare you for what is coming next in virtual reality. The future of virtual reality could be written by you!

Part One

Chapter 1. The first chapter was a brief explanation of our new era called the Fourth Industrial Revolution. This new era will allow us to use artificial intelligence, robotics, and quantum computers. Additionally, we will move into an era where we will live in five realities:

1. The real reality (reality without augmented reality, virtual reality, or holograms).
2. Augmented reality.
3. Virtual reality.
4. Mixed reality.
5. Holograms.

This book focused on one of these realities called virtual reality.

Chapter 2. Chapter 2 started to dig into the topic of this book. As you learned, virtual reality will look to fundamentally change the way we work, worship, and travel.

Part Two

Chapter 3. This chapter helped you define the creation of a personalized immersive experience where a person will feel like they are in another place that is special to them. For example, their body may be in the hospital, but their mind (and heart) can be somewhere else. I call this a 360 personal experience.

Chapter 4. Chapter 4 provides you with six steps for creating your own 360 personal experience.

1. Recipients.
2. Theme.
3. Participants.
4. Environment.
5. Experience.
6. Delivery.

Chapter 5. The next chapter helped take what you learned in Chapter 4 and apply it to creating 360 personal experiences with your loved ones in times of great joy.

Chapter 6. Chapter 6 helped you create 360 personal experiences in times of difficulty.

Chapter 7. The last chapter in Part Two explored the possibilities of creating 360 personal dream board experiences. These experiences allow your primary recipient the opportunity to watch their own future.

A future where they can walk again, have ran their next 5k, celebrated their five years of sobriety, or hit their financial goal.

Chapter 8. Chapter 8 helped you understand the possibilities of virtually bringing someone from where they are to somewhere else in the community (park, place of worship). This one-size-fits-all 360 video is called a 360 community experience.

Part Three

Chapter 9. The next chapter took the conversation to another level by explaining the purpose, considerations, functions, and possibilities of a virtual reality department.

Chapter 10. Chapter 10 taught a hospital leader how to create a virtual reality department for their facility.

Chapter 11. The next chapter taught a hospice leader how to start a virtual reality department and grant virtual reality last wishes.

Chapter 12. Chapter 12 explored how a senior/assisted living leader can create their own virtual reality station.

Part Four

Chapter 13. Chapter 13 took this concept forward by showcasing how to utilize virtual reality in your public relations campaigns.

Chapter 14. The last chapter illustrated how easy it is to create virtual reality advertisements by creating 360 personal experiences to your target audience.

Support

A main goal for this book was to demystify virtual reality for you. In doing so, my main intention was to help you and your community start finding solutions from the toolkit of the of our new era. These new tools are new to all of us, and it is my life's work to support you. After reading this book, I am here to offer you five levels of support.

1. Family support. The Virtual Reality for Main Street Movement will happen one family at time. As each family shares their experiences in virtual reality, they will look to share this new reality with their local hospitals, spiritual organizations, community organizations, and the world.

- **Book's website and social media sites.** Visit the book's website for free online tools. Here's a list of what you will find.

  - How to videos.
  - Expert interviews.

- Equipment recommendations.
- Real life examples.
- Weekly blogs.

- **Links.**

  - **Website:** www.vrformainstreet.com
  - **Facebook:** facebook.com/vrformainstreet

2. Community support. As you learned throughout the book, virtual reality allows you to virtually visit the past. My support will also extend to helping your community efforts in preserving your local history. In this preservation, I will support your creation of 360 videos and virtual reality simulations of your downtown area.

Can you imagine reliving an old memory from your local downtown from twenty years ago? This isn't an old downtown picture hanging up in the local pub. A person in twenty years will don their headset and feel like they are living a day in the past.

This past is your present day.

3. Hospital, hospice, and senior/assisted living leaders. It is my lifelong calling to help support your initiatives that look to connect your patients/residents with their loved ones and with the outside world. I am looking forward to helping you explore the possibilities of your new virtual reality department.

4. Business leaders. This book allowed me the space to start a conversation with you about how you can unleash your ability to connect with your target audiences by creating a compelling story in virtual reality. I would love the opportunity to meet with you about helping your business explore this new medium for your business.

5. Spiritual leaders. As a spiritual leader, I am excited to work with you and your place of worship on deploying virtual reality in your multiple ministries and outreach programs.

Visit **www.vrformainstreet.com** for more details.

- Free getting started worksheets and videos.
- Gain new insights with weekly online group meetings.
- Scheduling a one-on-one consultation with me.

I wish you the best of luck.

Todd Brinkman

Todd Brinkman

Create Your Virtual Reality Department
Lead From The Front With The Heart

Our team will work with your healthcare or senior living facility to create a VR Department. This new department will help to differentiate you in the marketplace as a leader in innovative care. Here is our three-step plan to get started.

1. **What's Possible Meeting.** First, our team can will help your executive team explore the benefits of this new department. This two-hour meeting will help your team better understand a VR Department's possibilities for care and ROI.

2. **Evaluation.** The next step will be to explore the needs of your facility. From here, our team will present to you a business plan that will help you to decide if you should get started, shelve the project, or scrap the idea.

3. **Start Small And Think Big.** Third, our team will help create your first smaller project to help validate its potential use of care in your facility.

Schedule an appointment with our team today. Contact us **info@vrformainstreet.com**.

Acknowledgments

This book has been the journey of a lifetime. It is the culmination of thousands of conversations. I'm so grateful for the hundreds of people who have supported me along the way. To begin, I must thank the men in the Men's Ministry at the Rock Church in San Marcos, California. As I came back to God to find my calling, they were there to support me in the beginning and to help kick-start this book project.

I'm grateful for my family. I'm grateful for my brother Troy who bought my first book on neuroscience that helped me to think through this project's development. I couldn't have written this book without seeing how my older brother Tom uses his ability to find breakthroughs in technology. Of course, I'm grateful for my loving parents. Finally, my chance to say thank you for all those amazing years when I was kid.

As the book came to an end, I couldn't have finished it without the support of my editors, Larry Alexander and Tyler Tichelaar at Superior Book Productions. Their honest feedback and support helped me polish the words you have just read. Lastly, I'm grateful for my two coaches that helped me through the process. They are my peak performance coach Kim Yeater (kimyeater.com) and publishing coach Christine Gail (unleashyourrising.com). Their inspiration and motivation helped me wrap up a three-year project.

I reserve my biggest thank you to close the book. I give all the credit to Jesus Christ. With His grace, I was able to change my life from looking to survive to making a difference.

Resources

Key Terms And Definitions (for easy reference)

Connection Conundrum. As technology increases, our ability to deeply connect with others decreases. I have learned to understand this phenomenon as our connection conundrum.

Immersive Bridge. A personalized immersive bridge is a 360 degree experience that virtually brings a person to a place in the present day, to their own past, or to their own future.

Fourth Industrial Revolution. The possibilities of billions of people connected by mobile devices, with unprecedented processing power, storage capacity, and access to knowledge, are unlimited. And these possibilities will be multiplied by emerging technology breakthroughs in fields such as artificial intelligence, robotics, the Internet of Things, autonomous vehicles, 3-D printing, nanotechnology, biotechnology, materials science, energy storage, and quantum computing.[11]

Augmented Reality. Augmented reality (AR) is an interactive experience of a real-world environment where the objects that reside in the real-world are enhanced by computer-generated perceptual information, sometimes across multiple sensory modalities, including visual, auditory, haptic, somatosensory, and olfactory.[12]

---

11 Schwab, Klaus. "The Fourth Industrial Revolution: what it means, how to respond." World Economic Forum. Retrieved 2017-06-29. From Wikipedia: https://en.wikipedia.org/wiki/Technological_revolution#cite_note-14.
12 https://en.wikipedia.org/wiki/Augmented_reality.

Virtual Reality. Currently standard virtual reality systems use either virtual reality headsets or multi-projected environments to generate realistic images, sounds, and other sensations that simulate a user's physical presence in a virtual environment.[13]

Mixed Reality. Mixed reality (MR) is the merging of real and virtual worlds to produce new environments and visualizations where physical and digital objects co-exist and interact in real time. Mixed reality takes place not only in the physical world or the virtual world, but is a hybrid of reality and virtual reality, encompassing both augmented reality and augmented reality via immersive technology.[14]

360 Personal Experience. A 360 personal experience is a live or recorded immersive personal experience that brings a person virtually to an important place in their own present day, to their own past, or to their own future.

Primary Recipient(s). The primary recipient(s) is the person (or group of people) for whom the video is created.

Secondary Recipient. A secondary recipient is a person who views the 360 personal experience through the eyes of another. This immersive video gives secondary recipients special access into the lives of the primary recipient(s). Ultimately, the video allows the secondary recipient to virtually walk in the primary recipient's point of view to build empathy and better understand their past, present, and projected future.

Time Recipient. A time recipient is either the primary or secondary recipient who views this experience in the future to watch an event from their own past.

---

13 https://en.wikipedia.org/wiki/Virtual_reality.
14 https://en.wikipedia.org/wiki/Mixed_reality.

360 Personal Dream Board Experience. A 360 personal dream board experience is an immersive bridge to a person's past or future that helps their mind believe they can reach their goals.

360 Community Experience. A 360 community experience is an immersive 360 video created for a large group of primary recipients. These primary recipients can be a whole community or a large target marketing audience.

Virtual Reality Department. A virtual reality department is tasked with helping a hospital, hospice, senior/assisted living center, or other local organization that serves the residents of a community. This support will be to create and find pertinent, timely, and safe content to showcase at their facility. This content will include: 1. Create 360 personal experiences, 2. Create 360 community experiences, and 3. Identify safe virtual reality simulations. Next, this department will be tasked with safely delivering these experiences. This can be accomplished with the use of virtual reality stations.

Six Steps of 360 Personal and Community Experiences

1. 360 Recipients. The people who will watch your experience.

- **Primary Recipient(s):** Who is this 360 for?
- **Secondary Recipient(s):** Who else may watch the video?
- **Time Recipient(s):** Who will watch this video in the future to relive an old memory?

2. 360 Theme. What is the purpose of your experience?

3. 360 Participants. Who is in your video?

4. 360 Environment. Where are you virtually bringing your primary recipient?

5. 360 Experience. The recording and uploading of your video.

6. 360 Delivery. How will your primary recipient view your experience?

- Individual in-person.
- Group in-person.
- Medically assisted.
- Mailed.

About The Author

———

Todd Brinkman grew up in the Twin Cities and eventually ended up in Central Minnesota after finishing his bachelor's and master's degrees in advertising. Todd has spent twenty plus years in developing traditional and digital marketing campaigns.

In 2016, he moved to Southern California to start a new career in content management systems (CMS). This new position allowed him to travel the Western United States to learn about many of our modern technological innovations. These trade shows led him to find his calling in virtual reality.

After finding his calling, Todd set out a mission to help hospital patients virtually pray from their place of worship before treatment. This passion has led him to explore further how VR can support others in prayer, personal development, and education.

Virtual Reality for Main Street is the cumulative effort of four years of work and thousands of conversations with people throughout the country.

Learn more at **vrformainstreet.com**.

www.ingramcontent.com/pod-product-compliance
Lightning Source LLC
Chambersburg PA
CBHW031236050326
40690CB00007B/826

9 781944 335274